P9-ELF-698

ARIZONA Outdoor Guide

- plants and animals
- rocks and minerals
- geologic history
- natural environments
- landforms
- natural resources
- national forests
- outdoor survival

by Ernest E. Snyder

Professor Emeritus
Arizona State University

Golden West Publishers

Cover design by Bruce Robert Fischer

Photographs by the author, Ernest E. Snyder

Plant and animal illustrations by Jane Kolber

Central Arizona Project map courtesy United States Department of the Interior, Bureau of Reclamation

Salt River Project map courtesy Salt River Project

Animal illustrations on pages 43, 73, 93, 94 and 102 courtesy of Primer Publishers, 5738 N. Central Ave., Phoenix, AZ 85012, publishers of the "Easy Field Guide" series.

Physical hazards may be encountered in visiting areas of Arizona, particularly old mining localities. Land ownerships and road conditions change over the years. Readers should take proper precautions and make local inquiries, as author and publisher cannot accept responsibility for such matters.

Library of Congress Cataloging in Publication Data

Snyder, Ernest E.
Arizona outdoor guide.

Bibliography
Includes index.
1. Natural history--Arizona. I. Title.
QH105.A65S68 1985 508.791 85-11454
ISBN 0-914846-20-5

Printed in the United States of America

Copyright © 1985 by Ernest E. Snyder. All rights reserved. This book, or any portion thereof, may not be reproduced in any form, except for review purposes, without the written permission of the publisher.

Golden West Publishers
4113 North Longview Ave.
Phoenix, AZ 85014, USA

Contents

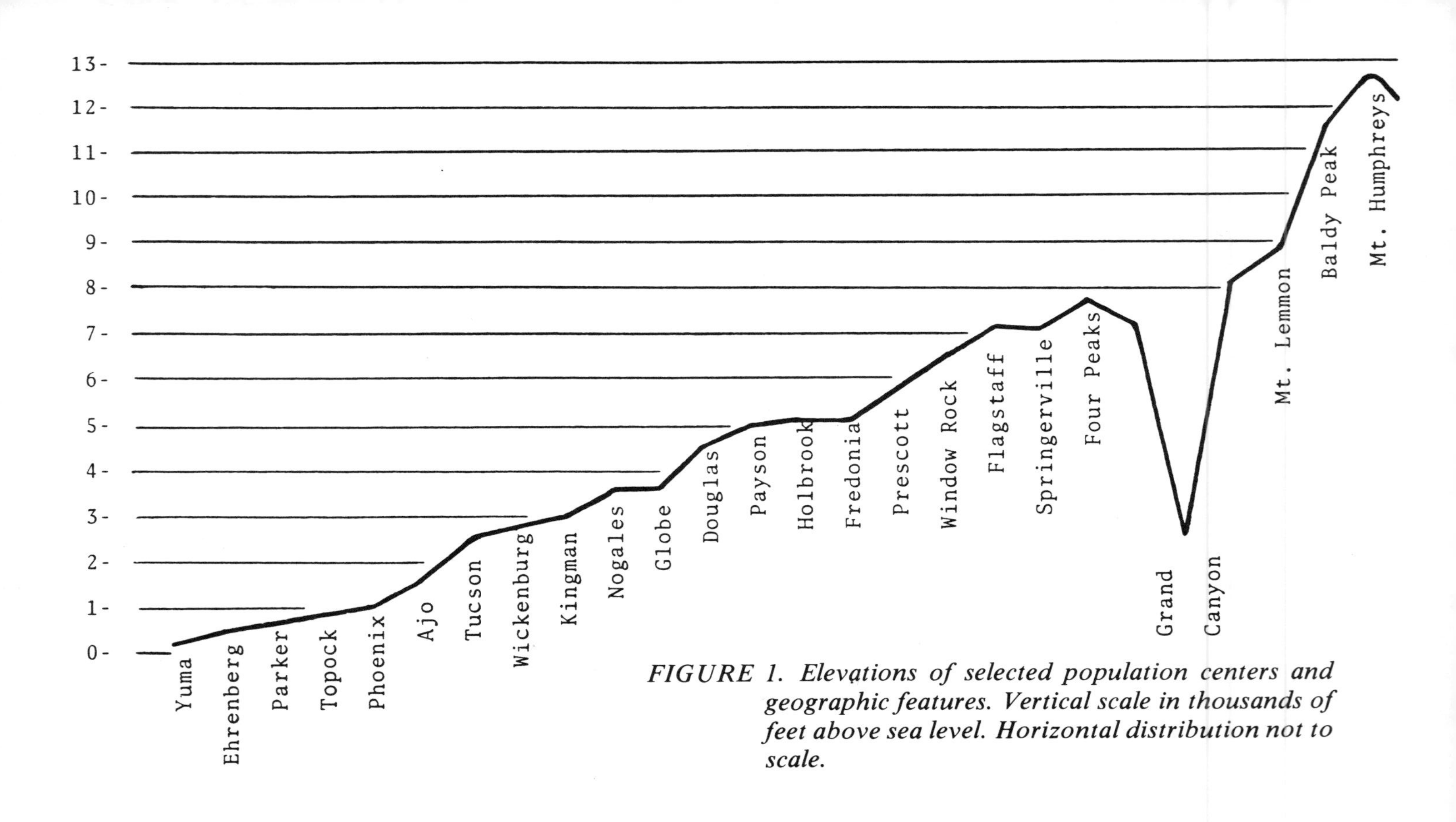

FIGURE 1. Elevations of selected population centers and geographic features. Vertical scale in thousands of feet above sea level. Horizontal distribution not to scale.

Introduction

Residents of Arizona are fortunate in that within a relatively short distance they can observe and study areas that are typical of many regions of the southwestern section of North America. What makes this possible are the pronounced changes in elevation above sea level and attendant annual precipitation and temperature that can be experienced by traveling in almost any direction for a relatively short time.

Surface elevations in the state vary from a few hundred feet above sea level at Yuma to more than 12,600 feet at the summit of the San Francisco Peaks near Flagstaff. Because of the effects of these changing conditions, one does well to develop the ability to think in several dimensions at the same time. Such matters as rainfall, snowpack, temperature, terrain, soil, drainage, insolation (sunshine), and ground cover combine to produce environments that make certain forms of life possible in a given area.

For the purposes of this publication, Arizona is divided into four ***physiographic provinces*** (Figure 2). A physiographic (or geologic) province is a region of the earth's surface whose landforms are more or less uniform within that region but are different enough from those of adjacent regions to permit easy recognition of the several provinces.

The four provinces ***(Basin and Range, Mountain, Transition and Colorado Plateau)*** are a compromise selection from a number of sources. *Each province is described in detail on subsequent pages.* It must be noted that these provinces do not terminate at the state line but extend into adjacent states and Mexico.

Changes in elevation are anything but uniform and this is the principal reason that we usually find several plant and animal communities in each province. Local variations in terrain and soil types and conditions also are important in determining the kind of biotic community existing in a given locality. Notable differences in plant communities may exist,

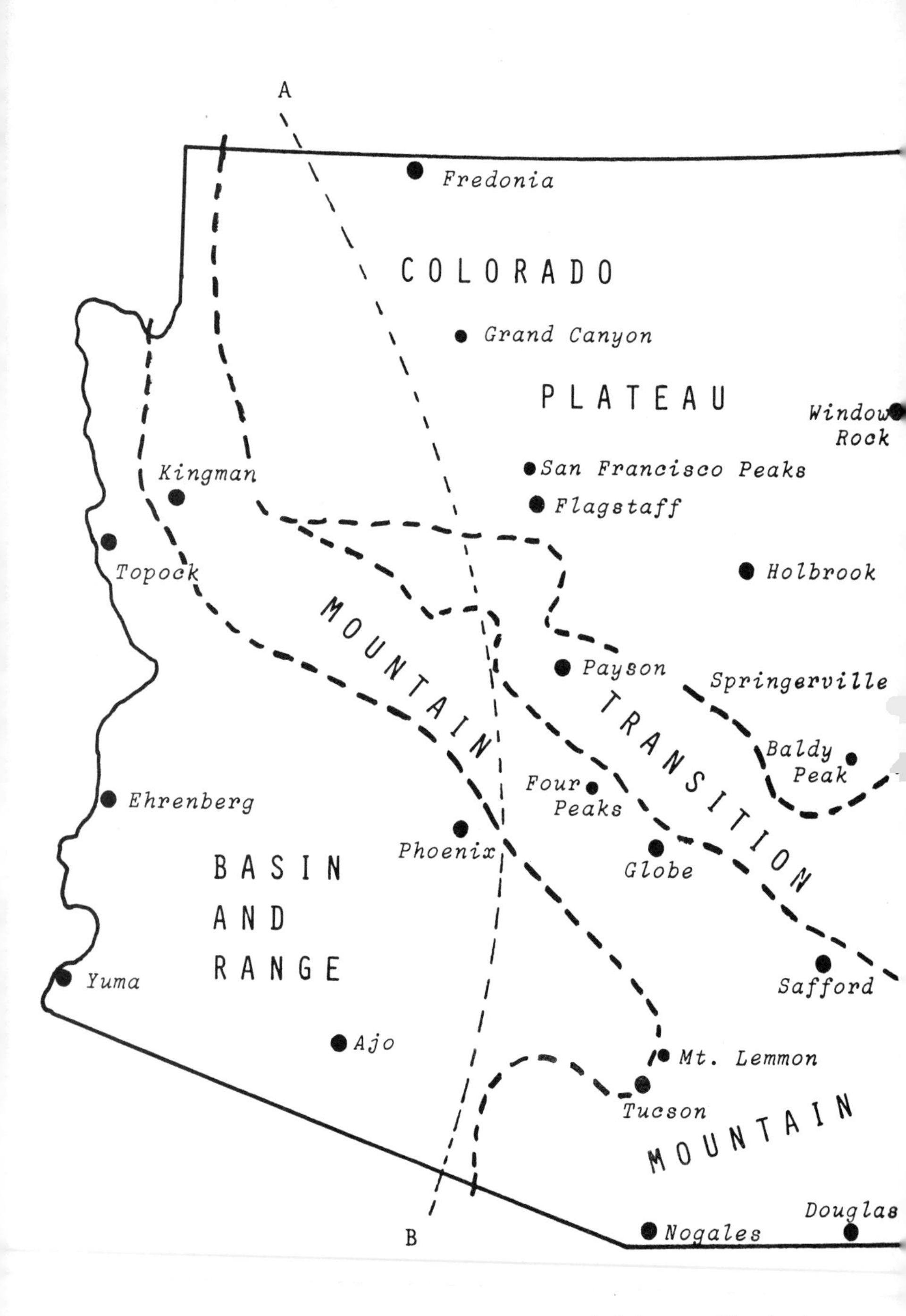

FIGURE 2. Physiographic provinces of Arizona. (Geologic cross section along line A - B appears in Figure 7.)

for example, on the north and south sides of a hill or mountain or on opposite slopes of an east-west oriented valley or canyon. Thus many "micro-communities" are found in the principal large communities listed below and described on following pages.

Figure 3 attempts, in a very general way, to relate moisture, elevation and temperature to the biotic communities. The communities found in the four provinces are listed here:

Basin and Range—Desert Shrub, Desert Grassland, Oak Woodland.
Mountain—Chaparral, Pinyon-Juniper, Ponderosa Pine, Pine-Fir, Spruce-Fir-Aspen.
Transition—Ponderosa Pine, Pinyon-Juniper, Pine-Fir.
Colorado Plateau—Pinyon-Juniper, Ponderosa Pine, Sagebrush Desert, Spruce-Fir-Aspen, Alpine Tundra.

In the following sections that deal with plant and animal life, only the more important communities and the most common species are discussed or mentioned. For a list of sources that provide much additional information beyond the scope of this work, the reader is referred to *Appendix A*.

The student and interested observer will detect many examples in the several biotic communities of:

Interaction and interdependence

All living organisms interact with other individuals and their environments. (See *Appendix C)* This interaction is especially evident in such things as food chains and food webs, territorial dominions, and competition for food, building materials, and living space. Interdependencies are illustrated by bees and flowering plants, algae and fungi (lichens), ants and termites, and various beneficial parasites.

Continuity and change

Everything in the universe is constantly changing. This is evident in the motions of all astronomic bodies and all living things, growth and death, weather, and sunset colors. And yet we see continuity in many things that are changing: day and night, all kinds of seasonal changes, life cycles, environmental

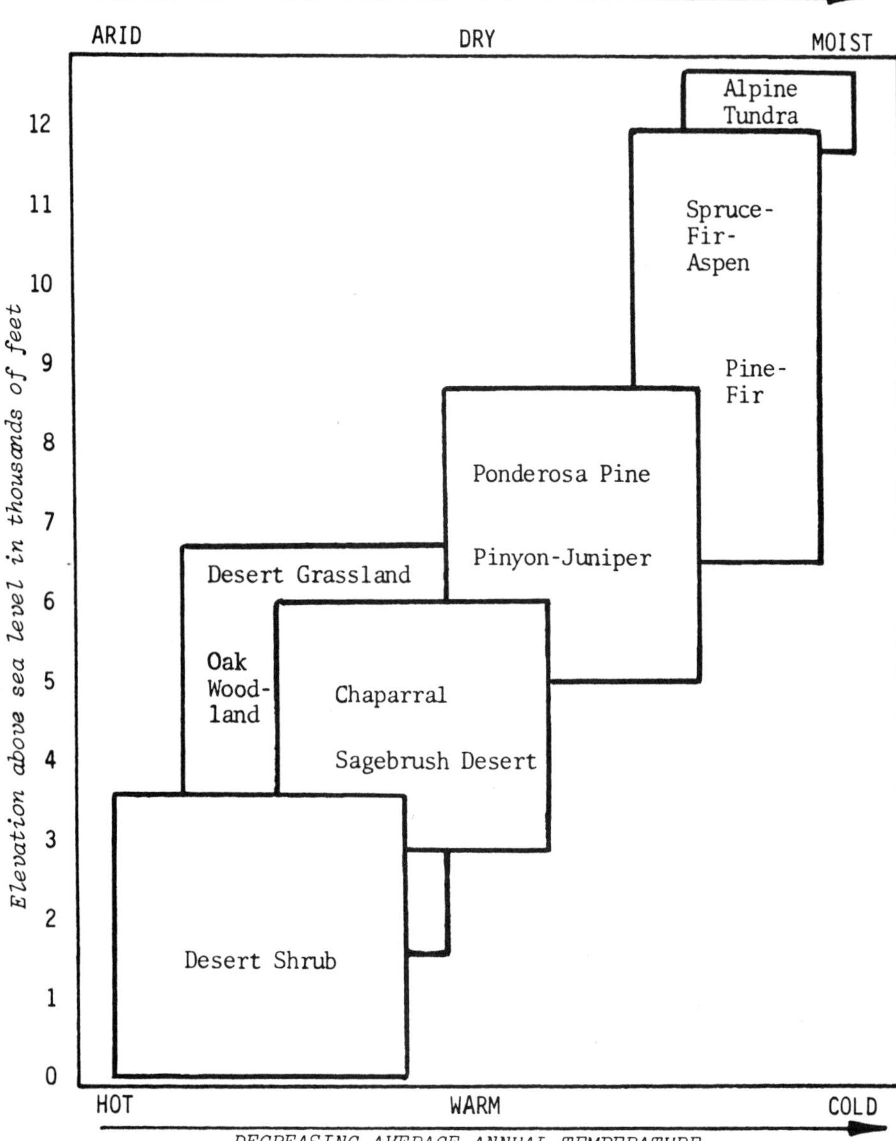

FIGURE 3. The general relationships between elevation, temperature, and moisture and the resulting biotic communities. Overlapping is due to local variations in environmental factors.

cycles (water, nitrogen, oxygen-carbon dioxide, rock, etc.), and circadian rhythms.

Variety and pattern

No two living individuals are exactly the same. Similarities and differences are apparent within and between species of plants and animals. Individual leaves on a tree may exhibit noticeable variety of form, but the general pattern is the same for the whole.

Evolutionary development and adaptation

These factors are apparent everywhere. The adaptations that desert plants have made in order to survive are discussed elsewhere in this book. Evidence of long-term evolutionary development in animals is seen in the fossils of extinct animals found now in the sedimentary rocks of the Colorado Plateau. Mountains are evolving from highlands to lowlands while other areas are being uplifted to form new highlands.

Aerial view of a desert range. Note how the outer slopes plunge abruptly beneath the surrounding plain.

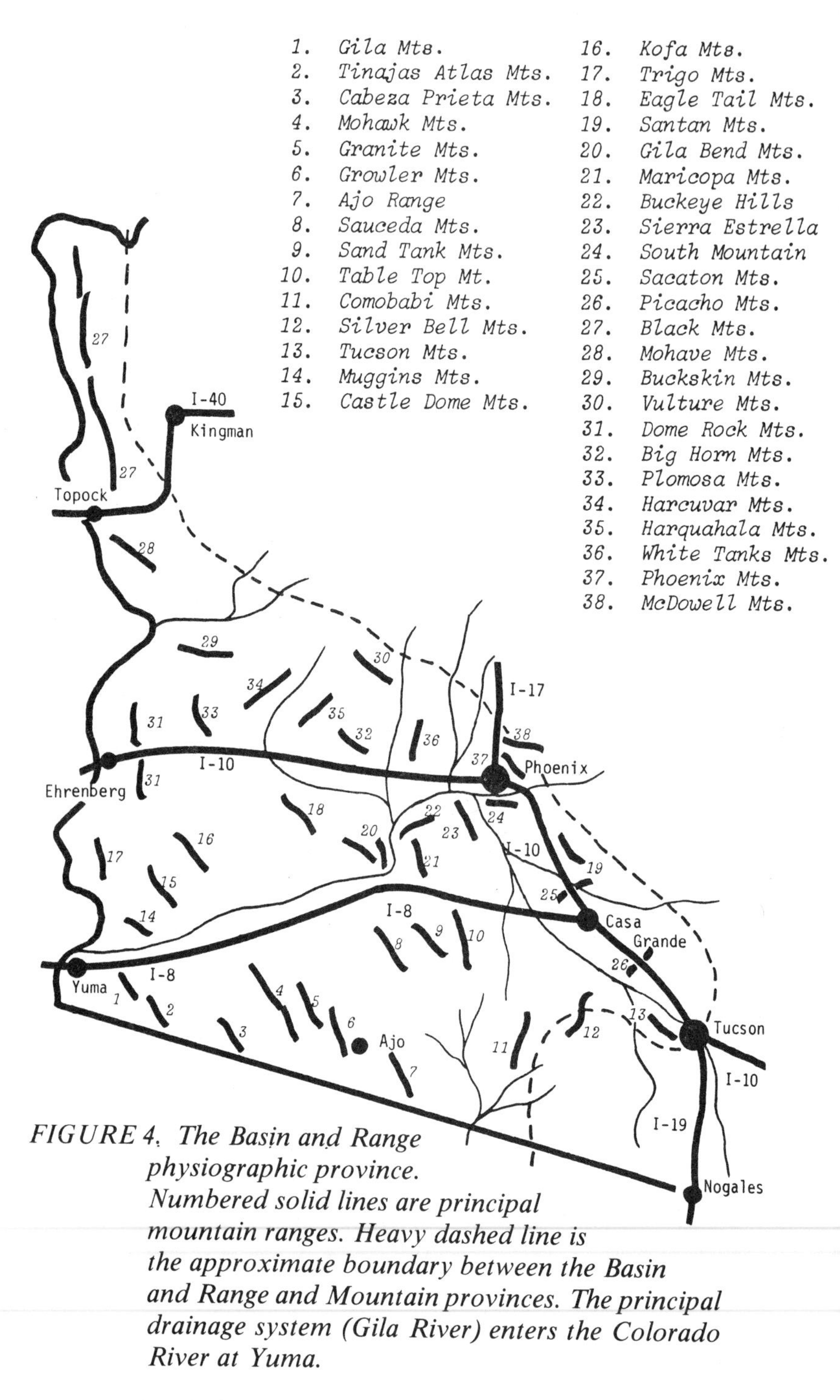

FIGURE 4. The Basin and Range physiographic province. Numbered solid lines are principal mountain ranges. Heavy dashed line is the approximate boundary between the Basin and Range and Mountain provinces. The principal drainage system (Gila River) enters the Colorado River at Yuma.

#1 Basin and Range Province

This province makes up about one-fourth of the state and incorporates most of the area lying between about 200 and 3500 feet elevation. It frequently is referred to as the "desert region." (See Figures 1, 2, 3 and 4 for areas and elevations.)

The Basin and Range physiography is characterized by a series of isolated mountain ranges that rise steeply out of a generally level basin floor. The basin floor is typically unconsolidated or weakly cemented gravel, sand and clay that was washed in from the surrounding highlands and the basin ranges themselves.

This area has been disturbed in the past in a manner that caused great blocks of the crustal rock to be elevated or depressed relative to each other. This ***block faulting*** is seen in the tilted aspect of the sedimentary remnants found here and there in the province. An example of this is Tempe Butte and the related formations that lie north of the butte across the bed of the Salt River (Fig. 5).

Here we find 4000 to 5000 feet of sedimentary formations that are now tilted about 45 degrees from their initial horizontal position. The oldest (lower) layers rest upon the ancient quartzite in Papago Park, and the upper (youngest) sedimentary rock is overlain by the more recent volcanic material that forms the summit and south side of Tempe Butte.

Another example of a sedimentary remnant in this part of the state is Red Mountain (or McDowell Mountain) at the southern end of the McDowell range and just north of the Granite Reef diversion dam near the confluence of the Verde and Salt rivers. The upper part and western end of the mountain is a red sandstone conglomerate that slopes toward the west. The eastern side is a basaltic lava flow. Other prominent sedimentary exposures occur in the Comobabi, Muggins, Buckskin and Rawhide mountains and in several areas very near Ajo, Yuma, Apache Junction and Wickenburg.

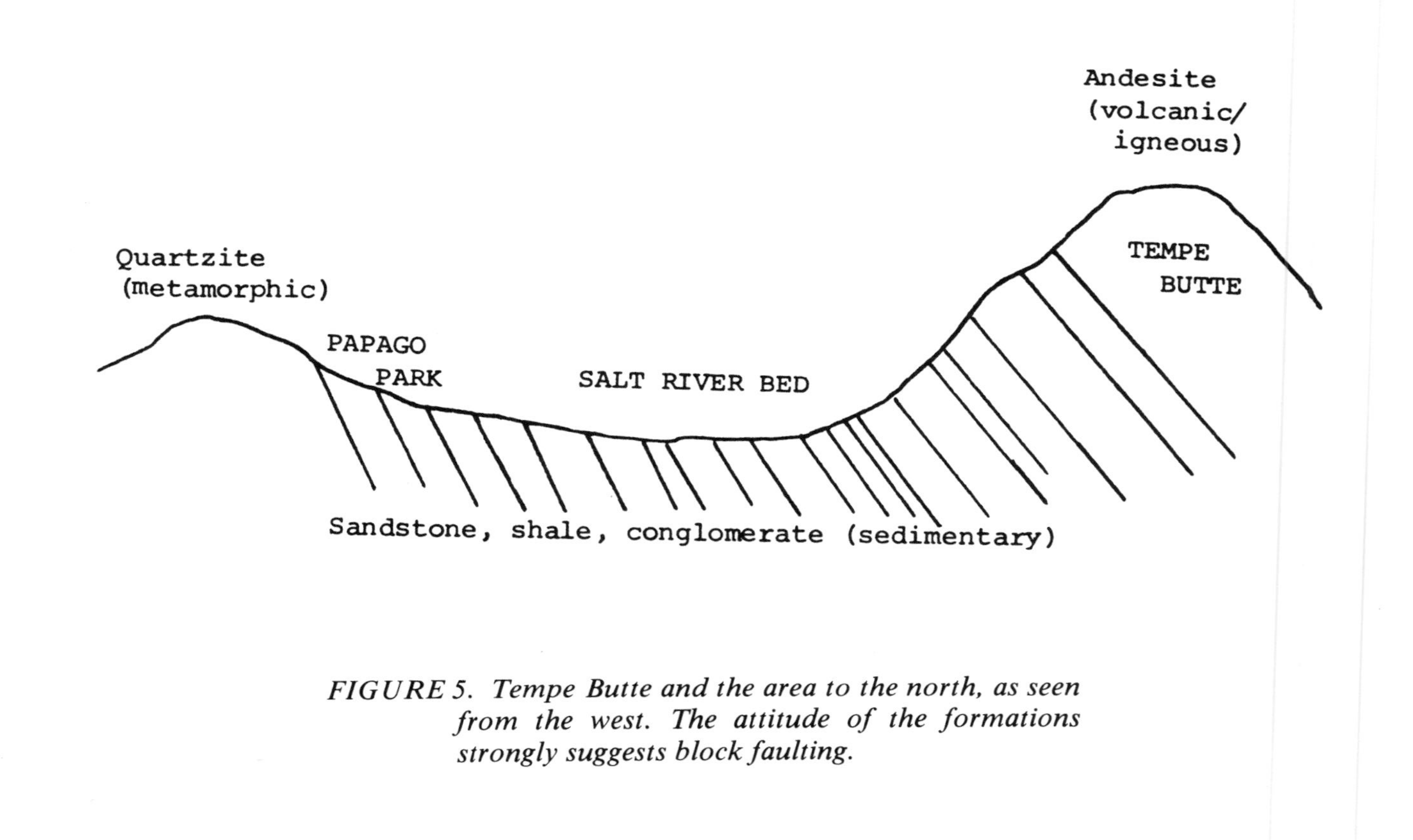

FIGURE 5. Tempe Butte and the area to the north, as seen from the west. The attitude of the formations strongly suggests block faulting.

Many basin mountain ranges appear to be the corners of great eroded blocks of the earth's crust projecting through the basin floor. This is especially evident when the area is viewed from the air.

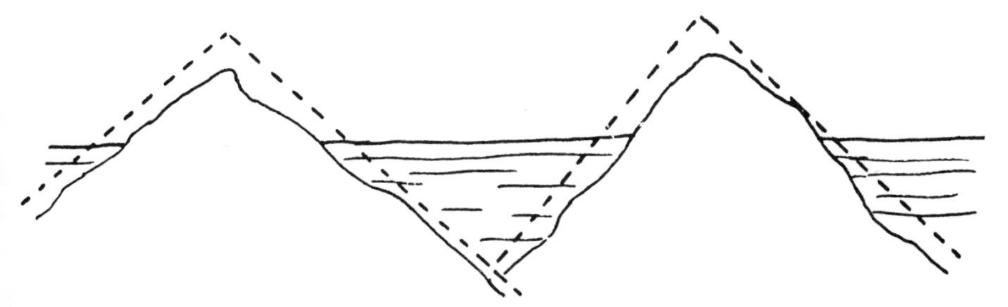

FIGURE 6. A vertical slice of the Basin and Range province might reveal the mountains as huge blocks of the earth's crustal formations exposed above the basin floor.

Basin ranges typically are long and narrow and sometimes occur in parallel groups (Figure 4). On the other hand, adjacent ridges may be aligned almost at right angles to each other as is the case with South Mountain and the Sierra Estrella (south and southwest of Phoenix) and the Harquahala and Big Horn mountains (south of Aguila).

A range may have one slope parallel to its longest axis that is much steeper than the opposite slope—another indication of the possibility of block faulting. Elevations of the mountains may range from a few hundred to several thousands of feet above the adjacent basin floor which usually is much wider than the ranges it separates.

The basin ranges consist predominantly of igneous and metamorphic formations. Granite, basalt, rhyolite, andesite, obvious volcanics (lava flows, plugs, dikes), gneiss, and schists make up the greater parts of these mountains. (See *Appendix B* for information about these kinds of rocks and formations.)

During the past 500 million years, the area that is now Arizona periodically was covered by an arm of an ancient sea. Sedimentary materials were weathered from adjacent land masses and deposited in the sea to eventually become sandstone, limestone, shale and conglomerate—to name the principal kinds of sedimentary rocks (*Appendix B*).

When the sea bottom periodically emerged and became part of the continental land mass, weathering and erosion proceeded in the same manner that we observe today. This area is presently in a period of emergence; the Colorado Plateau is almost two miles above sea level and still rising. Material is constantly being removed from the plateau and transported to the sea—or it was until the water storage dams were built along the Colorado River.

Evidence visible today suggests that what is now the Basin and Range province was once covered by extensive sedimentary formations. One may imagine that layers of rock similar to those making up the Colorado Plateau and Transition provinces once extended southward over the Basin and Range area but now have been broken up and largely removed by the usual geologic processes (see Figure 7).

Picacho Peak, a prominent Basin and Range landmark north of Tucson and close by Interstate 10.

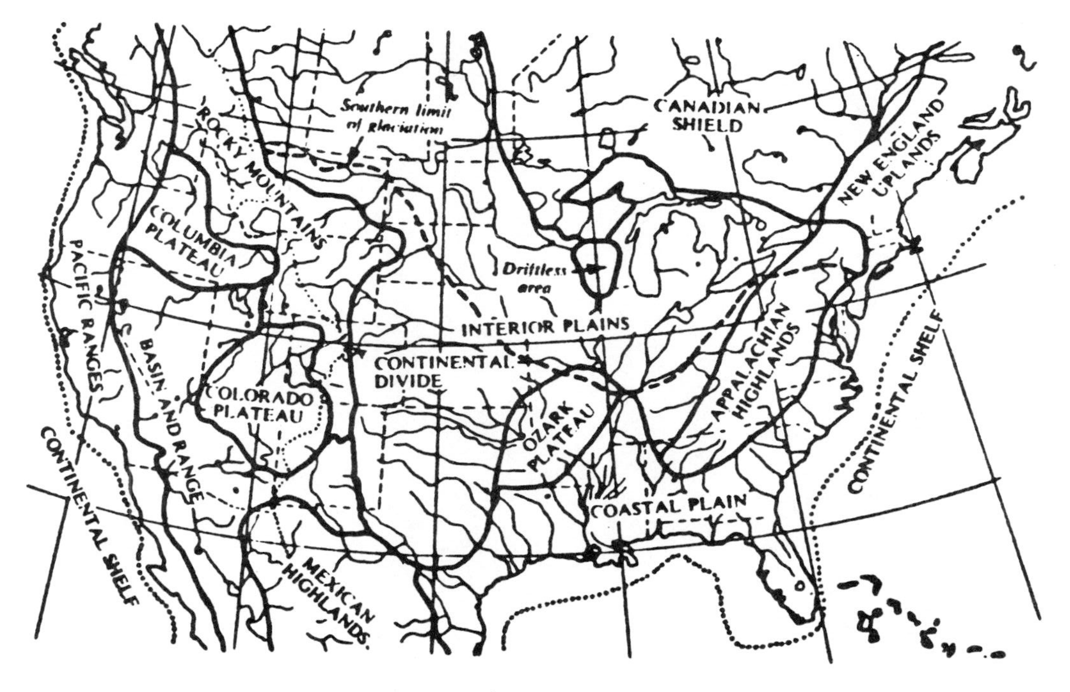

The principal physiographic provinces of the contiguous United States. Regional and local geomorphic variations often conveniently subdivide these large provinces. As in Arizona (see Figure 2).

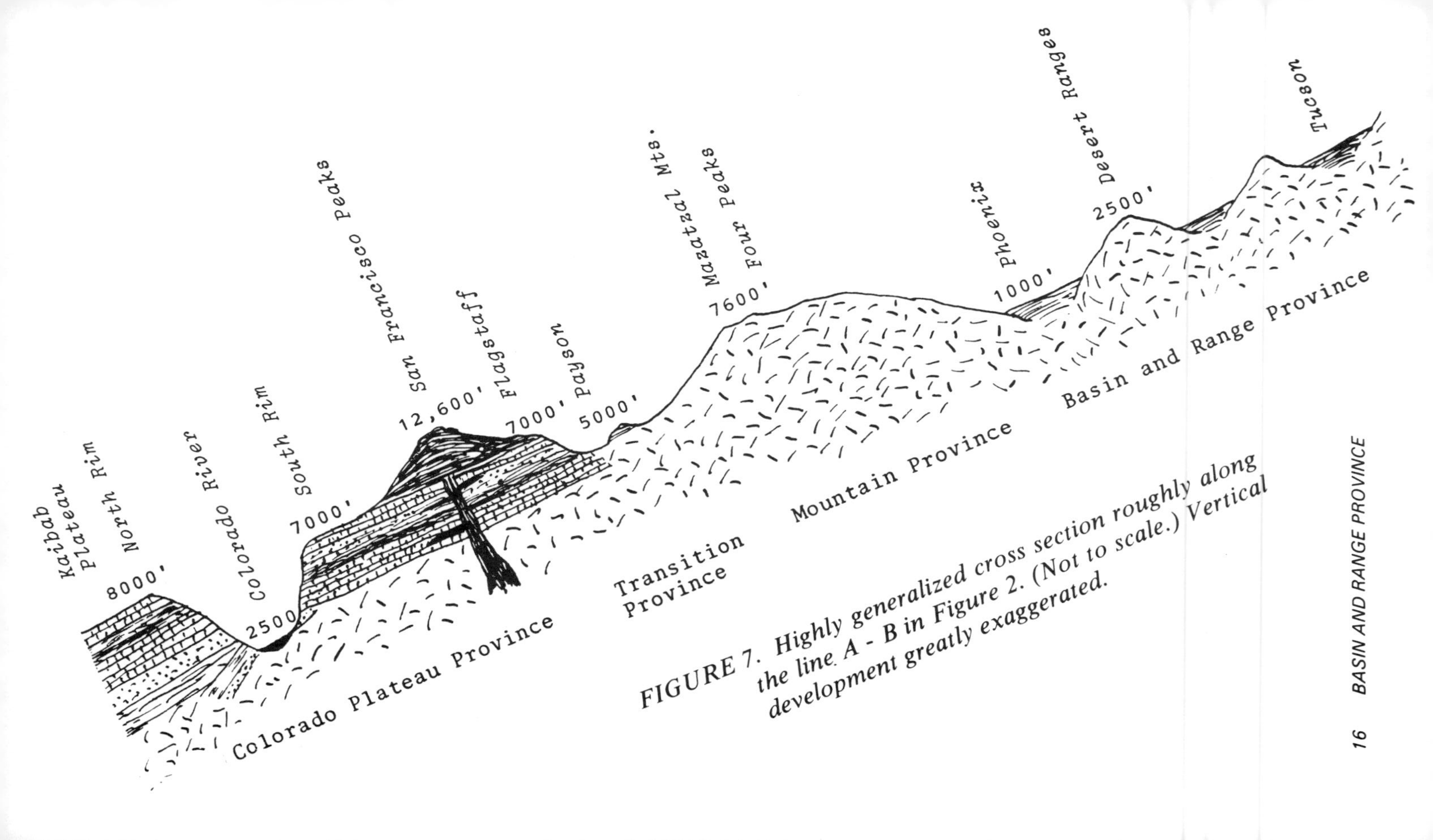

FIGURE 7. Highly generalized cross section roughly along the line A - B in Figure 2. (Not to scale.) Vertical development greatly exaggerated.

Salt River and Central Arizona Projects

The Salt River Reclamation Project in south-central Arizona was formed to provide irrigation water for the Phoenix area on a sustained basis. Before the construction of the first storage dam in the early 1900s, farmers and other residents of the area could not depend upon the flow of the Salt River to supply their needs. During the spring runoff of melting snow from the mountain watershed, the river would flood and wash out the brush and rock dams used to divert river water into irrigation canals. During the hot summer months, however, the river's flow would drop to an almost useless trickle at the very time that the water was most needed.

The answer to the problem was to build a series of storage dams on the Salt and Verde rivers to store the spring runoff for use during the remainder of the year. Four storage dams were built on the Salt and two on the Verde (see Figure 8).

These dams, their completion dates and capacities are:

Salt River: Granite Reef Diversion dam (1908), no storage. Roosevelt (1911), Roosevelt Lake, 1,336,700 acre feet*. Mormon Flat (1925), Canyon Lake, 57,800 af. Horse Mesa (1927), Apache Lake, 245,100 af. Stewart Mountain (1930), Saguaro Lake, 69,700 af.

Verde River: Bartlett (1939), Bartlett Lake, 178,100 af. Horseshoe (1945), Horseshoe Lake, 131,400 af.

These storage reservoirs supply most of the domestic and agricultural water for the Phoenix metropolitan area and the

*An acre foot is the volume of water needed to cover one acre to a depth of one foot. It is about 43,500 cubic feet or 325,850 gallons.

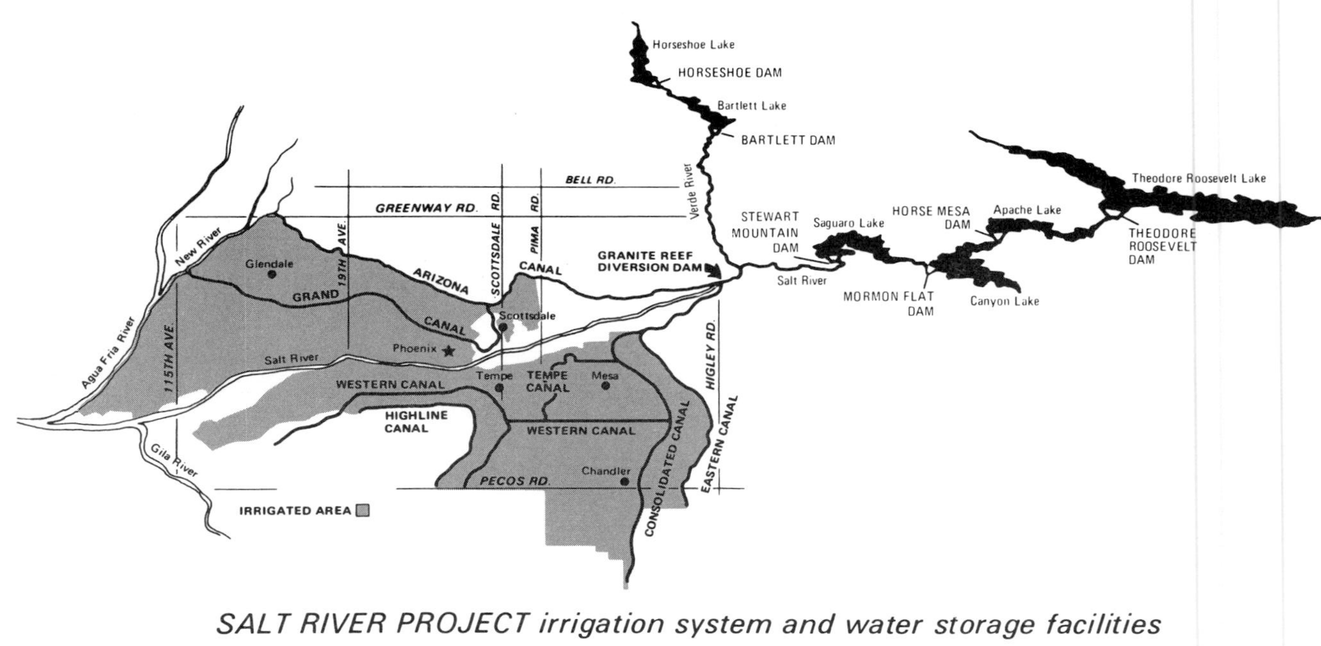

SALT RIVER PROJECT irrigation system and water storage facilities

surrounding irrigated farmland. The surface water is supplemented by pumping ground water from about 250 wells throughout the project service area. Most of the wells are located along SRP canals and the pumped water is discharged directly into the canals. The function of the Granite Reef diversion dam is to divert water coming down from the storage dams into two principal canals. These are the Arizona Canal on the north side of the river and the South Canal on the south side of the river. These two canals feed all the other Salt River Project canals. Because Granite Reef has no storage capacity, floodwaters pass over it into the normally dry Salt River bed below the dam.

Although the Salt River Project was not designed or charged with the responsibility for controlling flooding on the two river systems, it functions voluntarily in this regard during flood emergencies. In normal years, the lakes behind the dams accommodate the spring runoff. In years of excessive runoff, controlled amounts of water are released from the lakes to flow down the Salt River bed through the Phoenix area. Much of this water eventually finds its way to the Pacific at the Gulf of Cortez.

In February, 1980, the runoff into the SRP reservoirs hit a peak of 285,000 cubic feet per second—more than 390 acre feet per minute! By carefully regulating the flow into and through the storage lakes, the SRP was able to keep downstream floodwaters to 180,000 cubic feet per second.

Major electric generating stations are built into the four storage dams on the Salt River. As water moves through penstocks in the lower parts of the dams, its energy is used to turn turbines that power electric generators. SRP has expanded its power production to include ownership of all or part of 10 fossil fuel power plants and has 17 percent interest in the Palo Verde Nuclear Generating Station (located 50 miles west of Phoenix). The sale of electricity helps pay for the cost of storing and distributing water.

Most of the rest of the southern portion of the state that lies outside of the SRP service area must rely upon water pumped from the ground. Tucson, for example, is the largest city in the

United States whose sole source of water is pumped groundwater. As water is removed from below ground, some areas of the Basin and Range Province are slowly subsiding. In some places the elevation has changed as much as 30 to 40 feet in recent years. It is thought that the large earth cracks that have appeared here and there are the result of this settling.

The Central Arizona Project is designed to bring water from the Colorado River and distribute it in portions of Maricopa, Pinal and Pima counties. Presently under construction at an estimated cost of more than $3.5 billion, the project will consist of:

1. A pumping plant a short distance upstream from Parker Dam on the Colorado River. Water will be lifted more than 800 feet to the 6.5 mile-long Buckskin Mountain Tunnel. Electricity for the pumps is to be supplied from Hoover Dam and the Navajo generating plant near Page, Arizona.

2. The Granite Reef Aqueduct will carry water from the tunnel, a distance of 190 miles, to the Phoenix area. Three pumping stations will be located along the aqueduct at the Bouse Hills, Little Harquahala Mountains and the Hassayampa River. These stations will lift the water an additional 400 feet. Total lift from the Colorado River: 1200 feet.

3. The original plan called for building Orme Dam just below the confluence of the Salt and Verde rivers a few miles northeast of Mesa. Among other things, this would have inundated the Fort McDowell Indian village. Latest revisions eliminate Orme Dam in favor of several smaller storage dams on the Verde and Agua Fria rivers.

4. The Salt-Gila and Tucson Aqueduct will carry water from the Phoenix area to agricultural areas in Pinal and Pima counties and will supply domestic water to the Tucson area. This aqueduct will require four pumping stations to lift the water to the higher elevations along its route.

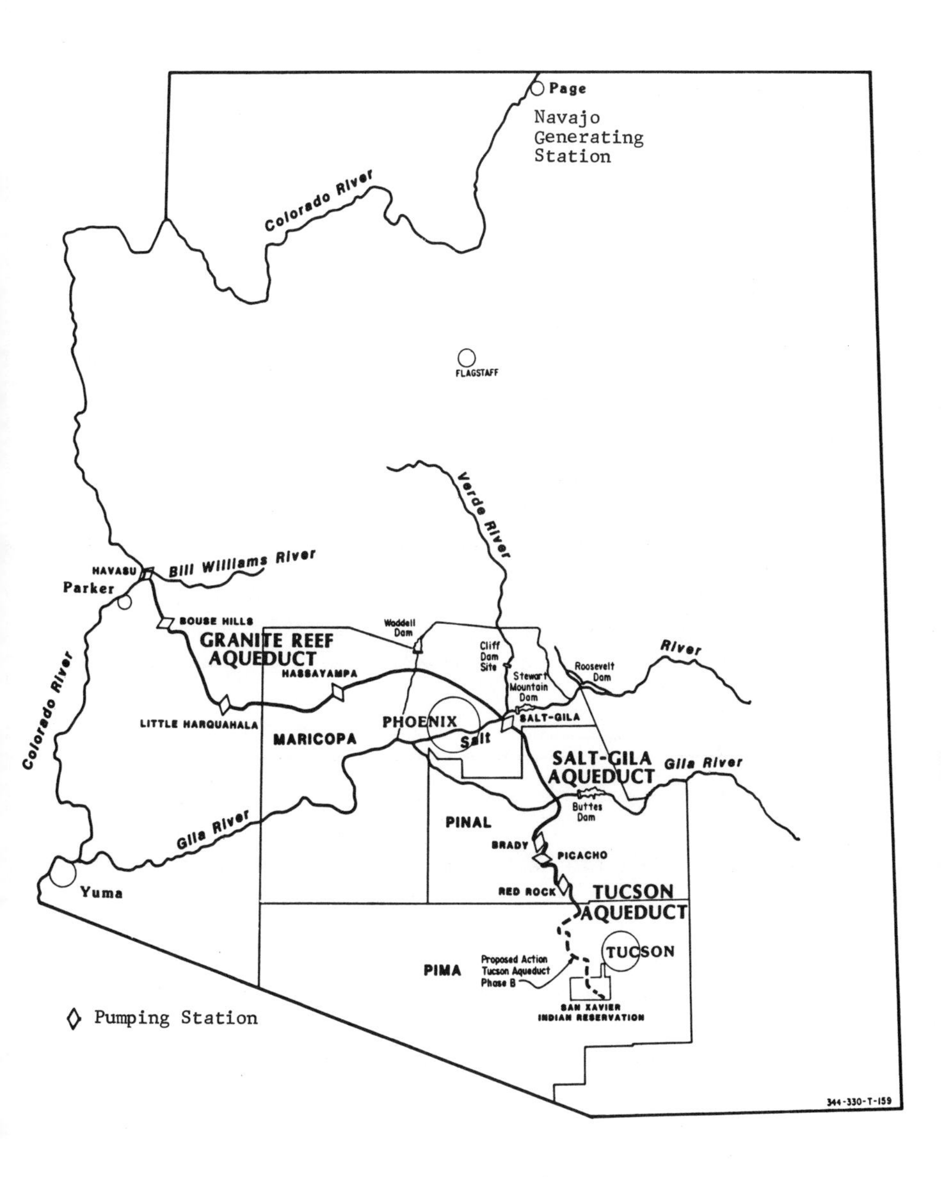

FIGURE 8. Locations of the principal parts of the Central Arizona Project. The Salt River Project dams and the Navajo Generating Station also are shown. (Map from Bureau of Reclamation publication, ***Central Arizona Project.****)*

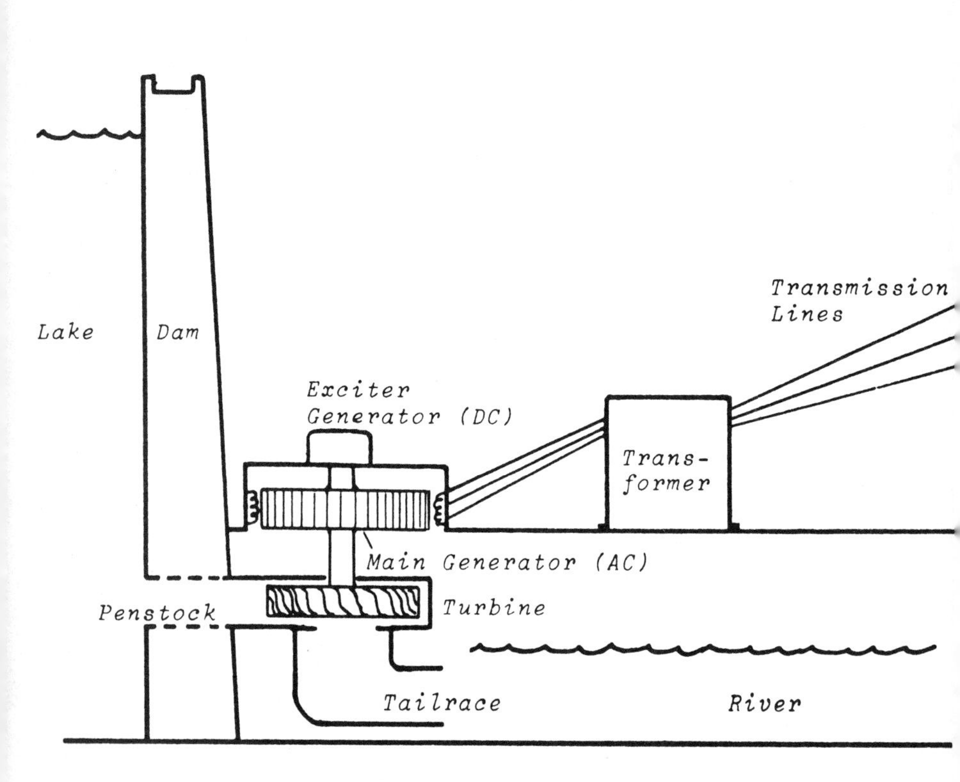

FIGURE 9. Diagram of a typical hydroelectric installation. (Not to scale.) The exciter generator turns with the main generator and supplies direct current electricity to the electromagnets located on the periphery of the armature of the main generator. Water under pressure behind the dam moves through the penstock and turns the turbine (water wheel) which rotates the generator armatures. The transformer increases the voltage before the electricity is sent through transmission lines.

•

Roosevelt Dam. The oldest and largest of the Salt River Project storage dams. (Photo page 23)

Desert Shrub Biotic Community

The principal plant community within the Basin and Range province is ***Desert Shrub*** referred to regionally as ***Sonoran Desert*** type vegetation. Within the main community are numerous variations that might be considered sub-communities. Usually this is a matter of one or several plants being dominant in a locality while different species dominate another area. Prominent examples include the very common creosote bush-bursage association in many areas and the paloverde tree-saguaro cactus community found in many places on well drained hillsides and along washes.

In any region where the precipitation averages seven inches or less per year, the variety and abundance of plant and animal life are understandably limited. On the other hand, the Sonoran Desert is not the sandy, barren wasteland envisioned by many who have not visited it.

All plants living under desert conditions have adapted to those conditions by one or more evolutionary developments: reduced leaf area, specialized leaves, ability to drop leaves (deciduous), vestigial or replaced leaves, shortened life cycle. Examples of the more prominent Desert Shrub plants in these categories are here listed and briefly described.

REDUCED LEAF AREA

Mesquite trees

Small, compound leaves. Older bark dark and rough. Inconspicuous yellow-green leaves. Good firewood for cooking.

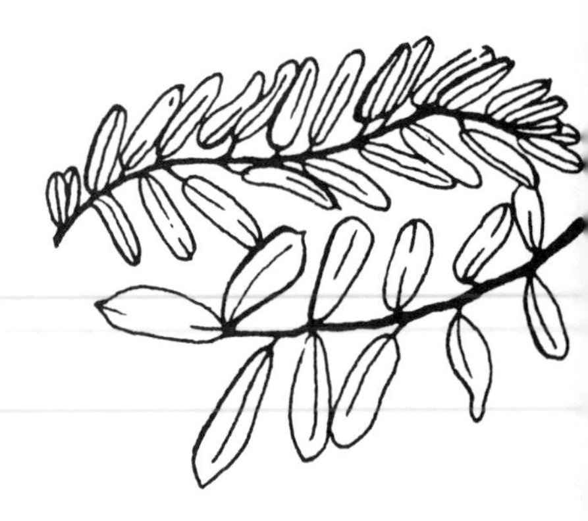

Ironwood tree

Leaves very similar to mesquite. Bark mostly smooth, light gray. Showy, lavender flowers in spring. Good firewood.

A Mesquite tree about 15 feet tall. The tree is deciduous and is just beginning to leaf out.

Ironwood tree. This one is in full leaf and about 25 feet tall. The wood, even when well-seasoned, will not float in water.

Paloverde tree

Leaves similar to others but much smaller and very sparse. Bark of trunk, limbs and twigs is green and has taken over most of the normal functions of leaves. Twigs terminate as long green thorns. Yellow flowers cover trees in spring. Arizona state tree.

All of these low-growing trees are found along washes and some grow on hillsides. The mesquite has a wider distribution than the others and frequently is found growing close to permanent water that is generally shunned by the paloverde and ironwood.

Catclaw

Shrub-like tree. Leaves and bark similar to ironwood. Thorns, however, are sharply curved where those of other trees are straight.

Bursage

Low growing shrub of wide distribution. Small leaves are covered with tiny hairs to minimize transpiration. Olive colored leaves vary in shape among the several species.

A Paloverde tree. The tiny leaves are not visible in the photograph. Height about 20 feet.

SPECIALIZED LEAVES

Creosote bush

Shrub with main woody stems branching at ground. Wide distribution over the Southwest; grows almost everywhere in Desert Shrub community. Leaves are quite small and coated with a resinous material having odor of creosote and acting as a transpiration retardant. Small yellow flower. Fuzzy gray fruit.

Yucca

Low-growing (branching from ground) or tree-like. Leaves a foot or more long, dagger-shaped and leathery with fibers peeling back along margins. Lily-like whitish flowers on a central stalk.

Jojoba

Higher elevation shrub. Leaves relatively large but with thick, leathery surfaces that reduce transpiration. Produces an edible nut.

A large Creosote bush—nearly 12 feet tall. This plant, along with the Bursage seen here at the base of the shrub, is widely distributed in the Sonoran desert.

One of several Yuccas common to the Arizona desert, this group is nearly head high.

DECIDUOUS PLANTS

Cottonwood tree

Grows only along permanent watercourses or where abundant water is very near the surface. Mature trees 60 or more feet tall. Found along streams, rivers and irrigation canals generally throughout the Southwest.

Willow trees

Small trees found along watercourses and some washes. Long, narrow leaves are characteristic.

Ocotillo

Higher elevation woody shrub that may grow 15 feet tall. Greenish brown stems covered with spines bear small leaves following rains. Leaves are dropped during dry spells. Showy red flower spike at tips of branches.

Brittle bush

Low shrub with light olive colored leaves grows abundantly on rocky slopes and along roadsides. Prominent yellow flowers project slightly above foliage and form conspicuous masses in early spring. Does not always drop all of its leaves in winter dry season.

Giant Cottonwood tree growing in town near irrigation canal. Desert trees do not usually grow as tall or as wide.

Ocotillo. Sometimes mistaken for a cactus when leafless. May reach 15 feet.

VESTIGIAL OR REPLACED LEAVES

Many desert plants have reached the point where leaf surfaces have ceased to exist as such and have been replaced by thorny or spiny structures. In other cases the leaves are vestigial, inconspicuous bracts. In some instances, a plant may have a combination of these evolutionary developments, but these fine points are of little interest except to the specialist.

In the several species of ***Cacti*** found in Arizona, stems have taken over all photosynthesis and most other functions. The generally abundant thorns serve to protect the plant and to shade the green stem.

Although Cacti are found over most of the Desert Shrub region, a given species may be restricted to a specific habitat. The teddybear cholla, for example, is found abundantly only in a rather narrow elevation belt and individuals that grow outside of those limits are exceptional.

Saguaro cactus

The giant trademark of the Sonoran Desert. May grow 50 or more feet tall and live one or two centuries. White, waxy flower is the state flower of Arizona. Prefers gravelly, well-drained hillsides. Fruit red. Spines straight, buff to black when mature.

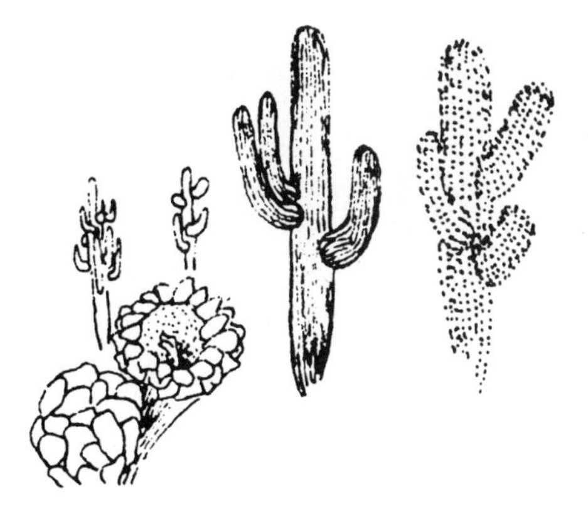

Barrel cactus

Older plants much shorter than the saguaro. Seldom branches. Spines pink or yellowish, longest ones flattened and curved at tip. Most individuals lean slightly toward the south. Flowers yellow or orange-yellow.

Cristation occurs in several species of the cacti but is not commonly seen outside of arboretums and desert gardens. This saguaro is a good example of a crested cactus. Hypotheses as to the cause range from radiation to birds pecking at the growing tip.

Barrel cacti leaning slightly toward the south. Note woody Saguaro skeleton lying in background.

Hedgehog cactus

Low-growing clumps usually not more than 1 ft. high. Individual stalks covered with long, straight spines. Flowers very showy lavender-purplish-red. One species (Rainbow cactus) has short spines and bands of different colors on stem.

Pincushion cactus

A number of species of *Mammalaria* are common in the Desert Shrub community. Best known is the fishhook pincushion. Growing only a few inches tall, it is identified by the long black spines curved on the end like a fishhook. Lavender flower, small red fruit.

Pricklypear cactus

Most widely distributed of all the Cacti. Characteristics common to Arizona species include flattened stem segments (pads), growth in large clumps, yellow to pinkish flowers, and large reddish-purple edible fruits.

Christmas cholla cactus

Low-growing shrub-like with joints about the thickness of a pencil. Yellowish inconspicuous flower. Fruit bright red, abundant, persistent in winter. Similar cactus with slightly thicker joints is the pencil cholla.

Teddybear Cholla cactus

Higher elevations. Medium height. Branches from a central stem. Joints densely covered with barbed, whitish spines. Segments are easily detached and take root under favorable conditions. Flower yellow, fruit green. Also called silver cholla and "jumping cactus."

Buckhorn, Staghorn, Cane Chollas

Similar in that broomstick thick joints branch out in the manner of deer antlers. May branch from ground or take on a tree-like appearance. Flowers red-purple or yellow-purple. Fruit yellowish.

Teddybear Cholla cactus. Not cuddly at all! Avoid all contact. Part of one of the Salt River lakes and a Mountain Province range in background.

Chain-fruit Cholla

Also called tree cholla and jumping cholla. Tree-like form may reach 15 feet or more. Small pink flowers. Green fruit is persistent and forms long chains that hang down from branches.

Diamond Cholla

Somewhat similar to the Staghorn cactus. Branches from ground. Joints covered with diamond shaped bumps (tubercles). Flower greenish yellow.

Mohave thorn. Frequently and erroneously called Crucifixion thorn. This specimen is about 12 feet tall.

Mohave Thorn

Resembles Paloverde with branches terminating in many green thorns. More shrub-like than tree-like, although it may grow 12-15 feet tall. No apparent leaves. Dark fruits may persist for several years. Occupies narrow elevation band between about 3500 and 4000 feet. Often listed as *Canotia.*

Mormon Tea (Brigham Tea)

Low-growing shrub. Plant seems to consist only of branching, greenish twigs, although there are scale-like leaves present. Yellow flower. Dried plant was used to brew a medicinal beverage by the Indians and early pioneers.

SHORTENED LIFE CYCLES

The ephemeral desert flowers that pop up with the spring or summer rains have adapted to the severe climate through their ability to live a fast life and die quickly.

Many of these plants go through a complete life cycle from germinating seed to the production of a new crop of mature seeds in a matter of only a few weeks. The seed crop (that part escaping seed-eating animals) lies dormant in or on the ground until conditions of moisture and temperature are again optimal. This usually means good rains in February and March on the desert. Seeds may lie dormant for several years before germinating.

Due to the uncertainty of their appearance and the brevity of their visits, the desert ephemerals are not listed here. Several sources for use in becoming acquainted with these plants are listed in *Appendix A*.

ANIMAL LIFE

Although human residents of the Desert Shrub community may observe and appreciate the relatively varied and abundant plant life, few are aware of the fact that animals in great numbers also are a part of that ecosystem.

One reason for this is that most people are out of the metropolitan areas and into the desert only as they drive along the highways. An occasional glimpse of a bird or a fourfooted animal is about all that one may hope to get under these conditions. Another factor is that most wild animals are nocturnal and seldom are seen under any conditions during full daylight hours.

To see the desert animals and to gain an appreciation for their numbers and variety, it is necessary to spend quiet time in the habitat. Early morning and late evening are good times and one may drive slowly along dirt roads after dark and see some of the more timid types of animals.

INSECTS

Most insects are vegetarians and most of the insect orders have representatives living in the Desert Shrub community. Many insects are not native to the community and live in and along the interfaces of human agricultural and urban environments that have intruded the desert.

Some of the Desert Shrub insects that depend primarily upon plants for food are: ***Grasshoppers*** and ***crickets*** (Orthoptera), ***termites*** (Isoptera), ***water bugs*** (Hemiptera), ***butterflies*** and ***moths*** (Lepidoptera), ***flies*** (Diptera), ***beetles*** (Coleoptera), ***ants, bees*** and ***wasps*** (Hymenoptera).

The desert insects generally are not unique. They fit into the organization of nature here pretty much as elsewhere. Although we are prone to connect the words "insect" and "pest," many insects in nature fill important useful functions: pollinating flowers, hastening the decay of dead organic matter, and providing essential links in food chains—to mention but a few.

MAMMALS

Most ***rodents*** subsist mainly on vegetable matter: nuts, seeds, berries, roots and the tender shoots of certain plants. The rodents form the chief link in the food web between plants and the predaceous animals of the desert ecosystem.

Some of the more common rodents found in the area are: ***Ground Squirrel, Rock Squirrel, Woodrat, Kangaroo Rat, Gopher, Porcupine*** (seldom seen in lower elevations), and several kinds of ***mice.***

These animals are able to survive and thrive in the harsh desert climate with a minimum of water. Some of them obtain all of their water from the solid foods they eat. Most of them burrow in the ground to escape the daytime heat and their enemies. The Woodrat heaps cholla cactus segments over his burrow to discourage unwanted visitors.

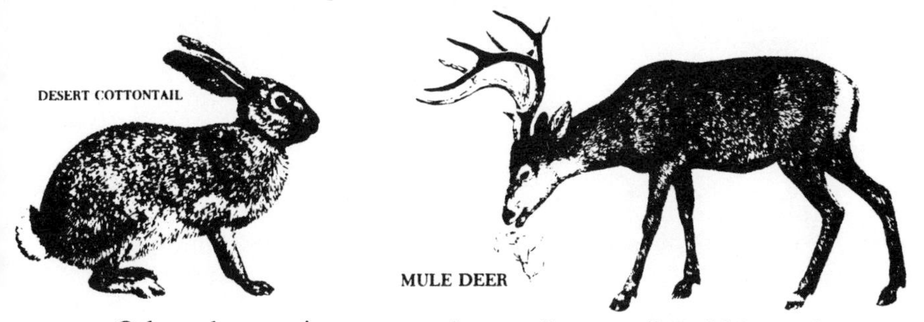

Other plant-eating mammals are: ***Cottontail Rabbit, Jack-rabbit, Desert Mule Deer, Sonora Whitetail Deer*** (Coues Deer), ***Javelina, Desert Bighorn sheep***, and certain nectar and fruit-eating ***bats.***

Desert mammals classed as predators are: ***Skunks, Coati, Ringtail Cats, Badgers, Foxes, Coyotes, Bobcats*** and the ***Mountain Lion*** (Cougar). Man's invasion of the natural communities housing these predators has brought about a drastic reduction in their numbers and a related disturbance of the balance of nature. One immediate result has been an alarming increase in the numbers of rodents which, in turn, is causing some serious alterations in the Desert Shrub community plants. (See *Appendix C* for more information about this phenomenon.)

BIRDS

Some common seed and insect-eating birds are: ***Cactus Wren*** (state bird of Arizona), ***Quail, Gila Woodpecker, Doves, Flycatchers, Thrashers, Flickers, Kingbirds, Hummingbirds, Mocking Bird, Swallows*** and ***Cardinal.***

The principal predatory birds are the ***Hawks, Eagles*** and ***Owls.*** Eagles are extremely rare, Hawks may be seen from any rural highway, and the Great Horned Owl and others seldom are found in full daylight and then are roosting far from the main highways. ***Roadrunners*** are predators that are frequently seen. They feed on vegetable matter as well as insects, lizards and small snakes. ***Crows, Ravens*** and ***Vultures*** feed on vegetation but prefer dead animals. They do not ordinarily kill.

REPTILES AND AMPHIBIANS

There are few amphibians in the Desert Shrub community other than in the neighborhood of permanent waters. About the only exception to this is the ***Colorado River Toad*** that can maintain itself under conditions that may be called only slightly moist. Several species of ***Frogs*** are fairly common in the permanent waters of the area.

A variety of lizards help keep the desert insect population under control. Among these are the ***Swifts, Geckos, Whiptails*** and the ***Chuckwalla.*** The ***Horned Lizard*** or Horned "Toad" sometimes is found in upper elevation areas. The only poisonous lizard is the ***Gila Monster***, which, like most other wild animals, is not dangerous if left alone.

The ***Desert Tortoise*** is a well-known member of the community and is found wherever there is green vegetation that they can harvest.

Snakes are not as numerous on the desert as some people would have other people believe. One is more likely to see the ***Western Diamondback*** or the ***Sidewinder Rattlesnake*** in the desert habitat than any of the non-poisonous kinds commonly found in the higher elevation communities. These snakes prey on small animals of all kinds but should not be expected to attack anything that they cannot swallow whole unless, of course, they are somehow provoked.

OTHER ANIMALS

There are a few animals inhabiting the Desert Shrub community that do not fit conveniently into any of the other categories:

Of the many ***spiders*** found in the desert, the best known are the ***Black Widow*** and the ***Tarantula.*** While the former is poisonous and is to be avoided, Tarantulas seldom bite people and when they do, the bite is more painful than toxic. The ***Brown Recluse*** also is poisonous and can be identified by the

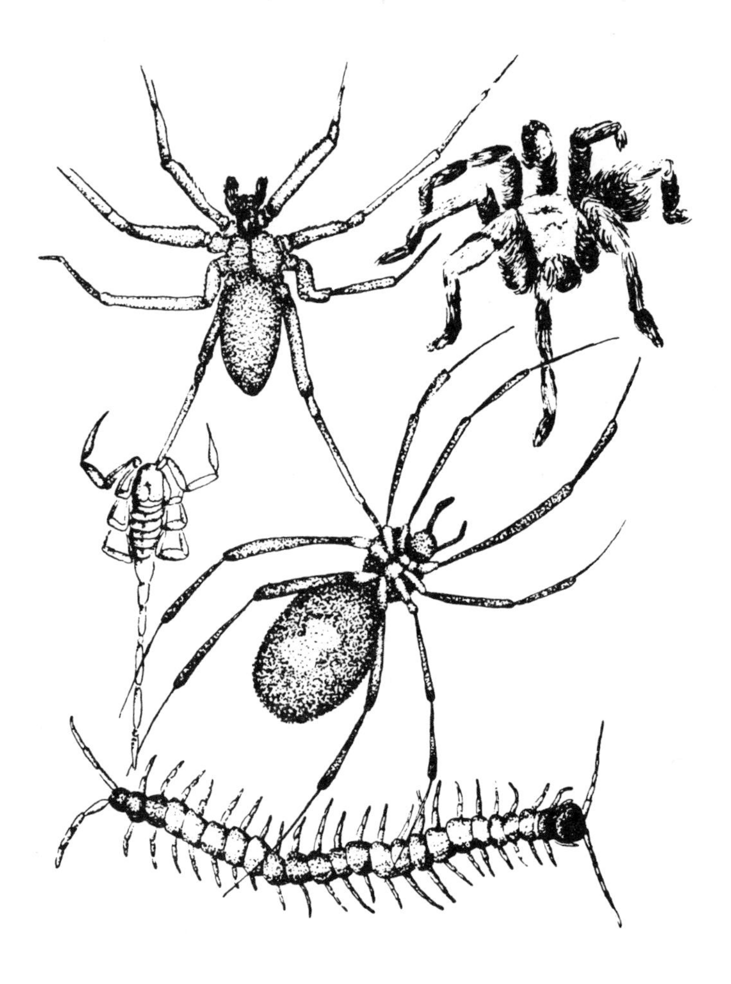

violin shape marking on its back.

The sting of the ***scorpion*** is poisonous and can be fatal to small children. These animals can be found anywhere but seem to prefer shelter under rocks, tree bark and dead plants. The so-called deadly species is smaller and slimmer than their larger and less venomous cousins. All are to be avoided.

The ***Giant Desert Centipede*** grows to a length of six inches or more. It may inflict a painful but usually harmless bite if handled.

#2 Mountain Province

The Mountain physiographic province is a belt of rugged mountain terrain about 50 miles wide that lies between the Basin and Range and Transition provinces. It overlaps and becomes interspersed with the Basin and Range province in the southeastern part of the state *(see Figure 2).*

Some authorities consider the Mountain province as part of the Basin and Range region. However, when the basin ranges are defined some of the larger mountainous masses in Cochise, Santa Cruz and eastern Pima counties seem to logically belong to the Mountain province. This accounts for the broadening of the province in the southeastern part of the state *(See Figures 2 and 10).*

The highest point in the province is Mt. Graham that lies a few miles south of Safford. While the elevation of Mt. Graham is an imposing 10,000 feet, most of the major mountain ranges do not exceed 8,000 feet above sea level. The lower elevations in this province are at 2,000 to 3,000 feet.

This province consists of a series of large mountain masses separated, for the most part, by pronounced canyons and valleys carved by the rivers and streams that traverse the region. Reading from northwest to southeast, the major mountain ranges making up the province are: *Hualpais, Junipers, Weavers, Bradshaws, Black Hills, New River Mountains, Mazatzals, Sierra Anchas, Superstitions, Pinals, Dripping Springs, Tortillas, Galiuros, Mescals, Gila Mountains, Pinalenos, White Mountains, Chiricahuas, Santa Catalinas, Tanque Verdes, Baboquivaris, Dragoons, Mule Mountains, Dos Cabezas (see Figure 10).*

Most of these mountain ranges appear to have been built up primarily as a result of a series of intrusions of granite and basalt into and onto overlying layers of sedimentary rocks. Subsequent faulting and erosion has resulted in the removal of most of the softer sedimentaries leaving igneous and metamorphic structures making up most of the province.

Because of the great variation in elevation, all of the plant

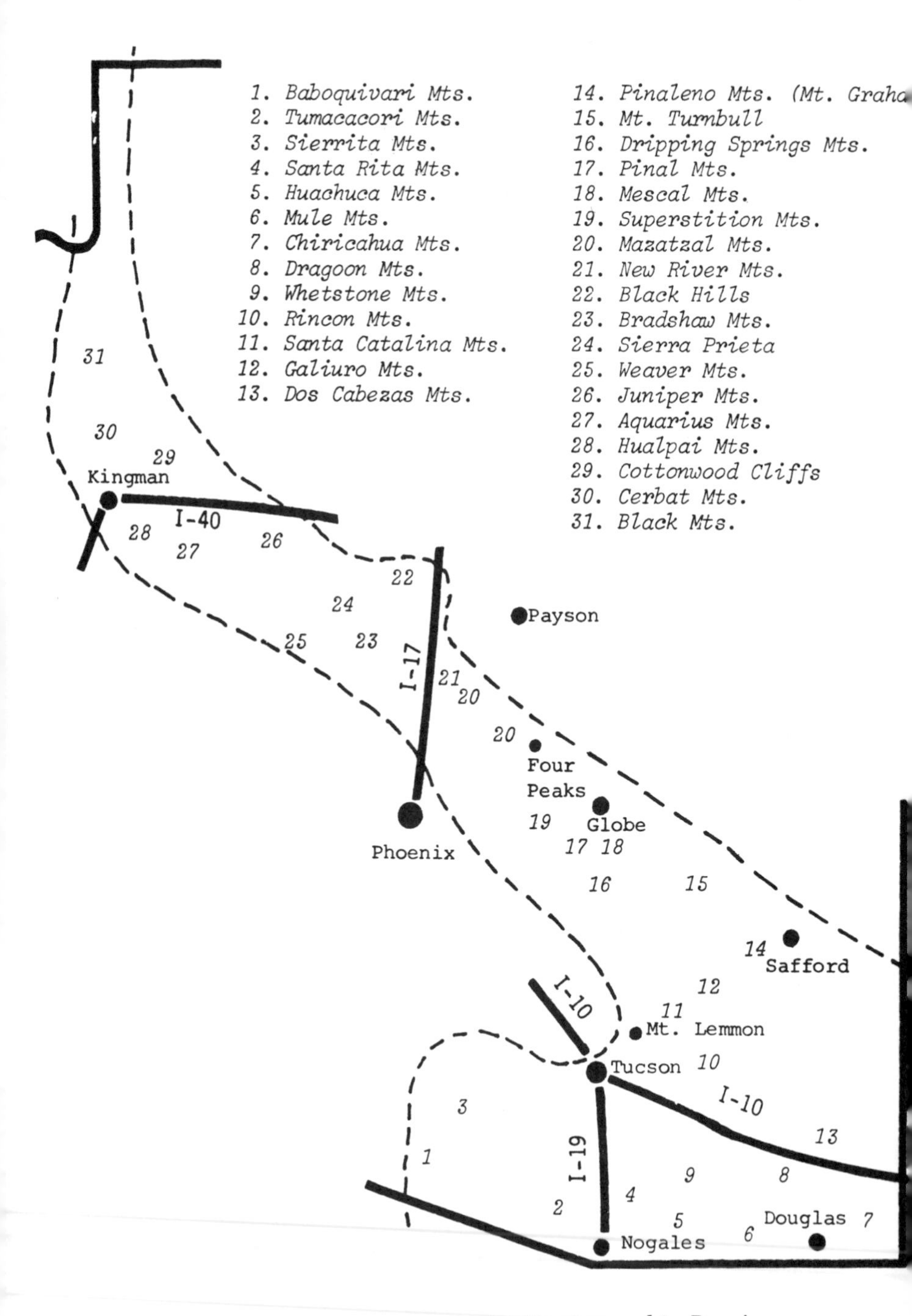

FIGURE 10. The Mountain Physiographic Province.

communities shown in Figure 3 (excepting Alpine Tundra) are found in this province. The dominant and most widespread communities, however, are ***Chaparral*** and ***Pinyon-Juniper.*** Areas of ***Ponderosa Pine*** and ***Pine-Fir*** are found in some canyons and near the summits of the higher mountains while ***Oak Woodland*** and ***Desert Grassland*** communities occupy foothill and valley regions in the southeast.

General Geology Along Principal Highways Through the Mountain Province

I—10 FROM TUCSON TO NEW MEXICO

Tucson to Mt. View: Loosely consolidated to unconsolidated sand, gravel and clay deposited not more than about 15 million years ago.

Mt. View to Benson: A few miles east of Mt. View, I-10 passes through a narrow band of conglomerates and, about halfway to Benson, some older (100 million years) sedimentary formations. Otherwise, you traverse the alluviums of the same sort as described between Tucson and Mt. View. The Whetstone Mountains south and east of Benson are, on the north end, Precambrian granite 2000 to 3000 million years old with the central portion being principally limestones of more recent origin *(Devonian and Mississippian - see Figure 11).*

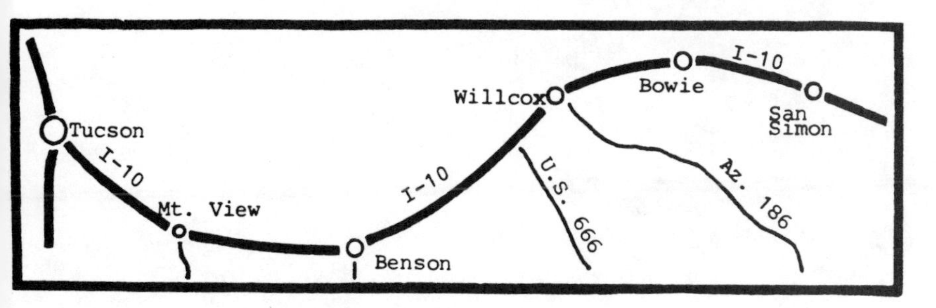

Benson to New Mexico: About 15 miles east of Benson the highway passes through the Little Dragoon Mountains over an area of Cretaceous intrusive granite. The Dragoon Mountains containing Cochise's Stronghold are visible to the south.

From here I-10 passes through more late alluvium deposits as it descends to the unconsolidated lake deposits of Sulfur Valley and the Willcox Dry Lake (Playa) south of the highway. A few miles east of Willcox I-10 passes between the Precambrian granitic masses of the Pinaleno Mountains to the north and the Dos Cabezas Mountains to the south. From Willcox to the New Mexico border, I-10 is almost constantly on the Pliocene alluvium mentioned earlier.

U.S. 60 FROM APACHE JUNCTION TO GLOBE

Apache Junction to Florence Junction: The fabled Superstition Mountain range to the north consists mostly of Cenozoic volcanic ash deposits that were subsequently consolidated (welded tuff). Despite their appearance, there are no sedimentary formations here.

Rugged Mountain Province terrain near the foot of Superstition Mountain.

An erosional remnant in the Superstition Mountain range.

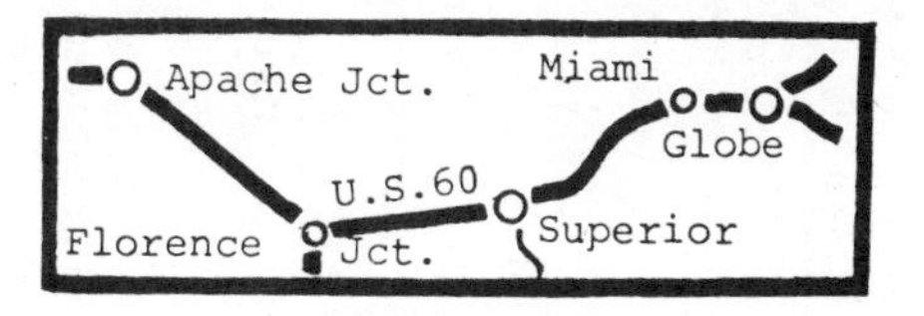

Florence Junction to Superior: Continuing ash deposit mountains to the north. Between Queen Valley road and Gonzales Pass there are many exposures of Precambrian schist. From the pass to the outskirts of Superior the highway is in another area of volcanics: dacite, tuff, rhyolite, andesite, basaltic lava flows. Picketpost Mountain adjacent to Boyce Thompson Arboretum is a good example of a layered volcanic mountain.

The Superior copper mining area is a complex of igneous (mostly volcanic) and sedimentary rocks. Apache Leap Mountain south of the town overlies the older sedimentaries and is capped by dacite (Cenozoic) that extends as surface

YEARS AGO	ERA	EPOCH OR PERIOD	EVOLUTIONARY AND OTHER EVENTS	ONE YEAR TIME SCALE
200	CENOZOIC		Industrial revolution	Dec 31, 11:59:59 PM
500			Columbus arrived in America	Dec. 31, 11:59:57 PM
5000			Agriculture developed	Dec. 31, 11:59;25 PM
600,000		Pleistocene	Modern plants, large mammals, man dominant	Dec. 31, 11 PM
2,000,000		Pliocene	Earliest form of man appeared	Dec. 31, 8 PM
11,000,000		Pliocene	Humanoid apes, mammals abundant	Dec. 31, 1 AM
25,000,000		Miocene	Mastadons, elephants, grazing animals abundant	Dec. 29, 6 PM
40,000,000		Oligocene	Primitive monkeys and apes, saber-tooth tiger	Dec. 28, 6 PM
60,000,000		Eocene	Modern mammals appear	Dec. 27, 4 AM
70,000,000		Paleocene	First primates, ancient mammals dominant	Dec. 26, 9 AM
135,000,000	MESO-ZOIC	Cretaceous	Flowering plants, extinction of giant reptiles	Dec. 20, 9 PM
180,000,000		Jurassic	Giant reptiles dominant, modern insects appear	Dec. 17, 3 AM
225,000,000		Triassic	Giant and mammal-like reptiles evolve	Dec. 13, 7 PM
270,000,000	PALEOZOIC	Permian	Extinction of many marine invertebrates	Dec. 9, 7 PM
330,000,000		Pennsylvanian	Scorpions, cockroaches, swamp forests, amphibians	Dec. 5, 7 PM
350,000,000		Mississippian	Sharks, crinoids common, insects evolving	Dec. 3, 7 PM
400,000,000		Devonian	Brachiopods, corals, fish dominant, first forests	Nov. 29, 7 AM
440,000,000		Silurian	First land plants and air-breathing animals	Nov. 28, 3 AM
500,000,000		Ordovician	Brachiopods, trilobites, first vertebrates	Nov. 24, 3 AM
600,000,000		Cambrian	Marine invertebrates and algae abundant	Nov. 17, 9 PM
1,700,000,000	PRECAM-BRIAN	Late	Worms, algae, sponges, bacteria, fungi	Aug. 13, 9 PM
2,600,000,000		Middle	Earliest life forms: fungi, blue-green algae	June 1, 9 PM
4,500,000,000		Early	No evidence of life, formative stage of Earth	Jan. 1

Adapted partially from Heller, Robert L., Editor, *Geology and Earth Sciences Sourcebook*, Holt, Rinehart and Winston, Inc., New York, 1962.

FIGURE 11. Geologic time scale including some events since humans became the dominant form of life on earth.

exposure for about eight miles east of Superior.

Superior to Globe: Between Superior and the Queen Creek tunnel, the road is in some of the limestones in which the copper is concentrated. Beyond the tunnel and extending all the way to Pinal Ranch near the summit above Miami, the road is on volcanic dacite as you travel through Queen Creek Canyon, Oak Flat and Devil's Canyon.

From Pinal Ranch to Miami, the surface exposure is almost entirely Cretaceous granite. The rounded boulders and surfaces are characteristic of granitic weathering.

Between Miami and Globe the surface material is unconsolidated or loosely welded alluvium materials (sand, clay, gravel).

U.S. 70 FROM GLOBE TO NEW MEXICO

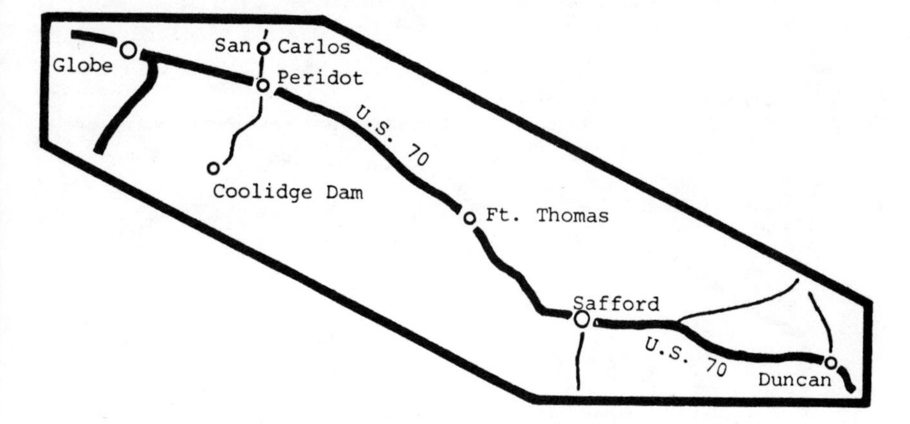

Globe to Bylas: Alluvium between the Gila River to the south and the San Carlos River watershed to the north. The highway passes through several areas of Pleistocene volcanics.

Bylas to Safford: Prominent peak to the southwest is granitic Mt. Turnbull (8280 ft.). Highway is on unconsolidated alluvium forming the flood plain of the Gila River. Gila Mountains to the north consist of volcanics and basaltic flows. The Pinaleno Mountains to the south of Thatcher and Safford are chiefly Precambrian granite with some schist and gneiss. Mt. Graham

(10,717 ft.) is the highest point in the range.

Safford to New Mexico: U.S. 70 leaves the Gila River flood plain a few miles east of Safford and goes through a minor volcanic mountainous area before reaching Duncan on the Gila River.

U.S. 60 FROM GLOBE TO SPRINGERVILLE

Globe to Salt River Canyon: Leaving Globe, the highway passes through several miles of alluvium and from this point to the Salt River Canyon it crosses alternating sections of basalt (diabase), unconsolidated alluvium, shales, quartzite, conglomerate and back into the diabase as the descent into the canyon begins.

The Salt River Canyon reveals the layered nature of this area. The escarpment just across the bridge on the north side of the river is quartzite. Above this is limestone, then basalt, and the cap rock at the top is more quartzite. Most of the sedimentary and metamorphic formations in the canyon were formed during the Paleozoic era.

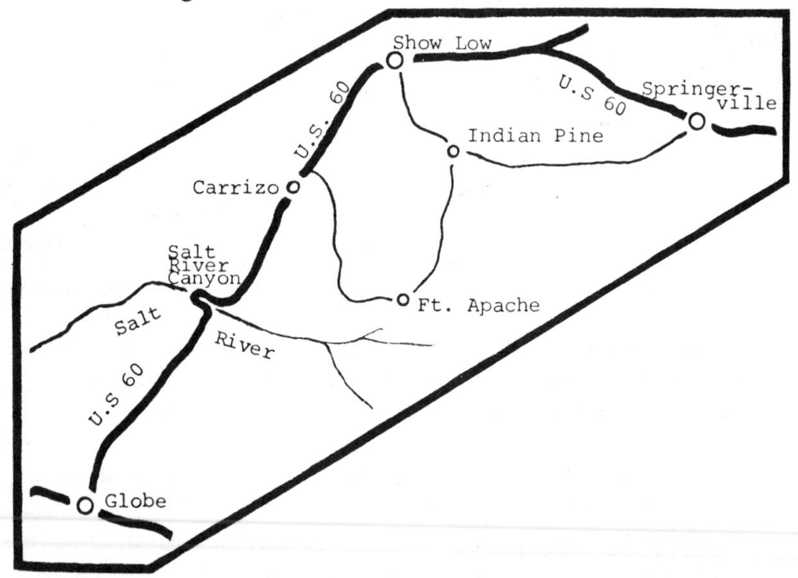

Salt River Canyon to Show Low: The highway tops out of the canyon onto some Colorado Plateau sedimentaries including

Mountain Province terrain in Slate Creek Canyon a few miles north of Sunflower on Arizona 87. The dwellings in the foreground no longer exist. This was a small mining town that functioned when mercury ore was mined and processed in the Mt. Ord area.

the Redwall limestone that is also exposed in Grand Canyon. After a few miles of alluvium, the road again crosses some sedimentary formations and, a mile or so north of Carrizo, enters an area of basaltic material that continues to within a few miles of Show Low. Here the short climb up the rim crosses the Paleozoic Supai formation, Coconino Sandstone, Kaibab Limestone, and a series of shales and limestones at Show Low.

Show Low to Springerville: Although this area is on the Colorado Plateau, it also is included in the White Mountain complex which is the result of extensive volcanic activity of only a relatively few million years ago that spilled lavas and ashes over the plateau and the area to the south. The White Mountains extend from Show Low and Springerville southward to Morenci and Safford and for some distance into New Mexico to the east.

The highway from Show Low to Springerville is continually in the volcanics that are typical of the area. The numerous cinder cones are ample evidence of the origin of the land forms. The higher mountains to the south all are of volcanic origin. At Springerville there is a small area of flood plain alluvium.

ARIZONA 87 FROM MESA TO PAYSON

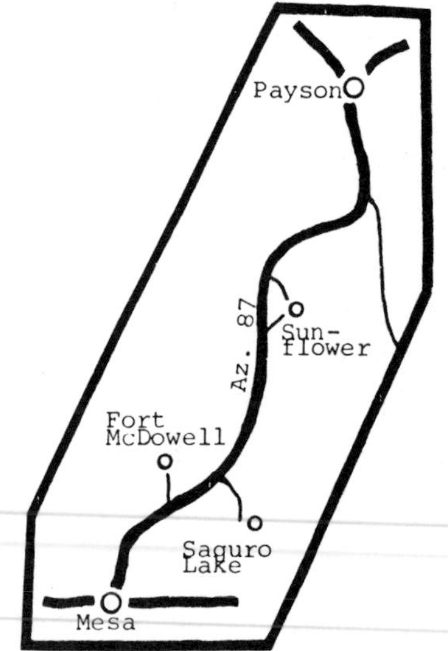

This highway heads north from McDowell Road between Scottsdale and Mesa. The first few miles to the crossing of the Arizona Canal is over unconsolidated alluvium of the flood plain of the Salt River to the east. Beyond the canal the route is through a low pass in the McDowell Mountains. Sawik Mountain to the west is an extinct volcano. Red Mountain on the east is the southern terminus of the McDowell range. The upper portion of Red Mt. is a sandstone conglomerate, while the lower portion on the south and east is basalt. In descending to the Verde River, the highway crosses about a mile of Precambrian granite.

From the Verde River to a mile or so beyond the U.S. Forest Service Desert Vista wayside, the roadbed is on alluvium almost continually. The granite mass of Stewart Mountain is visible to the right as you approach the Saguaro Lake turn-off.

Desert Vista affords a good view of the Mazatzal Mountain range (Four Peaks prominant) and the north side of the Superstitions.

A mile beyond Desert Vista there is a good view to the west of Sugarloaf Mountain—a volcanic erosional feature. The road climbs a granite ridge (note typical granitic weathering to rounded boulders) containing some interesting quartzite dikes ("rock walls"). Note the difference in color between the weathered granite and the relatively fresh surfaces exposed in some of the road cuts.

A large earth crack that suddenly appeared several years ago near Bush Highway east of Mesa.

From Sycamore Creek to Sunflower the highway is through volcanic and granitic areas entirely. Past Sunflower, the highway crosses the Mazatzal range and descends Slate Creek Canyon—an area of strongly metamorphosed sedimentary material. Slate, schists and shales predominate. This area once produced significant amounts of mercury from cinnabar, the sulfide of the metal (HgS). The mountain with towers atop and south of Slate Creek Canyon is Mt. Ord—a mass of Pre-cambrian schist and granite. From here to near Rye, the road traverses alluvium associated with the Tonto Creek drainage system (Tonto Basin lies between the Mazatzals and the Sierra Anchas mountains to the east).

From Rye to Payson the surface rocks are mostly Greenstone, a general term for metamorphosed volcanics, and granites of Pre-cambrian age. Payson is the southern edge of the Transition Province at this point and the Mogollon Rim that is the southern edge of the Colorado Plateau is seen to the north.

INTERSTATE 17 FROM PHOENIX TO CAMP VERDE

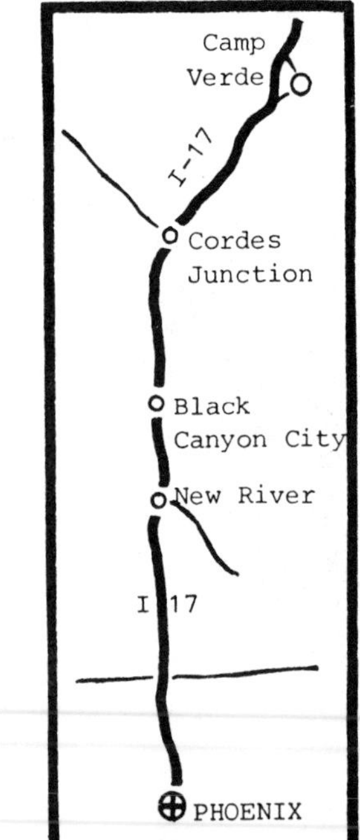

Phoenix to Lake Pleasant Turnoff: Highway is on basin alluvium (Pliocene) with andesite, basalt (Miocene), granite and schist (Precambrian) isolated hills and small mountains to right and left.

Lake Pleasant Turnoff to Black Canyon City: Once out of the basin alluviums, road crosses an area of schists and basalt. Two stretches of alluvium near New River and Black Canyon City are the result of erosion and deposition by the New and Agua Fria rivers. Interesting volcanic features are prominent to the east of the Black Canyon

City area and the Black Canyon itself is to the west as the highway climbs toward the top of Hutch Mesa.

Black Canyon City to Camp Verde: With the exception of a few alluvium deposits near streams and rivers (usually dry), the highway is entirely on the surface of the huge basaltic lava flow that caps large areas of the Mountain and Colorado Plateau provinces to the north, east and west. The New River Mountains to the east and the Bradshaws to the west protrude well above this basalt and themselves are predominantly granite and schist (Precambrian). The descent via Copper Canyon into the Verde Valley and Camp Verde brings one to the Transition province in this region.

Part of the erstwhile ghost town of Jerome, once a principal copper mining area in the state.

Minerals and Mining

Arizona produces a significant amount of non-ferrous minerals (copper, gold, silver, etc.), non-metallic minerals (sand, gravel, stone, asbestos, gypsum, etc.), mineral fuels (coal, oil, natural gas), and gem stones (agate, turquoise, petrified wood, amethyst, etc.). The dollar value of mining and processing these substances is second only to manufacturing in the state's economy. Arizona normally produces more than 50 percent of the copper mined in this country. Mineral production is listed here in terms of decreasing total value of the products:

Copper
Coal
Molybdenum
Sand and gravel
Silver
Gold
Zinc
Stone
Lime
Uranium
Pumice
Lead
Vanadium
Natural gas
Gypsum
Petroleum
Mercury
Clay
Gem stones

Copper accounts for about 85 percent of the total value of all minerals produced in the state. Several of the heavy metals (molybdenum, gold, silver, zinc, lead, platinum) are largely derived as by-products of processing copper ores. Very few operating mines are producing primarily gold or silver, since most of these were worked out many years ago.

Choice mineral specimens and semi-precious gem stones can be found at many localities in this state. Mine dumps frequently are good sources of interesting specimens. One should be cautioned, however, against entering abandoned mine tunnels and shafts. Many of these are just waiting to collapse on any intruder that might disturb rotting timbers or loose, unsupported rock.

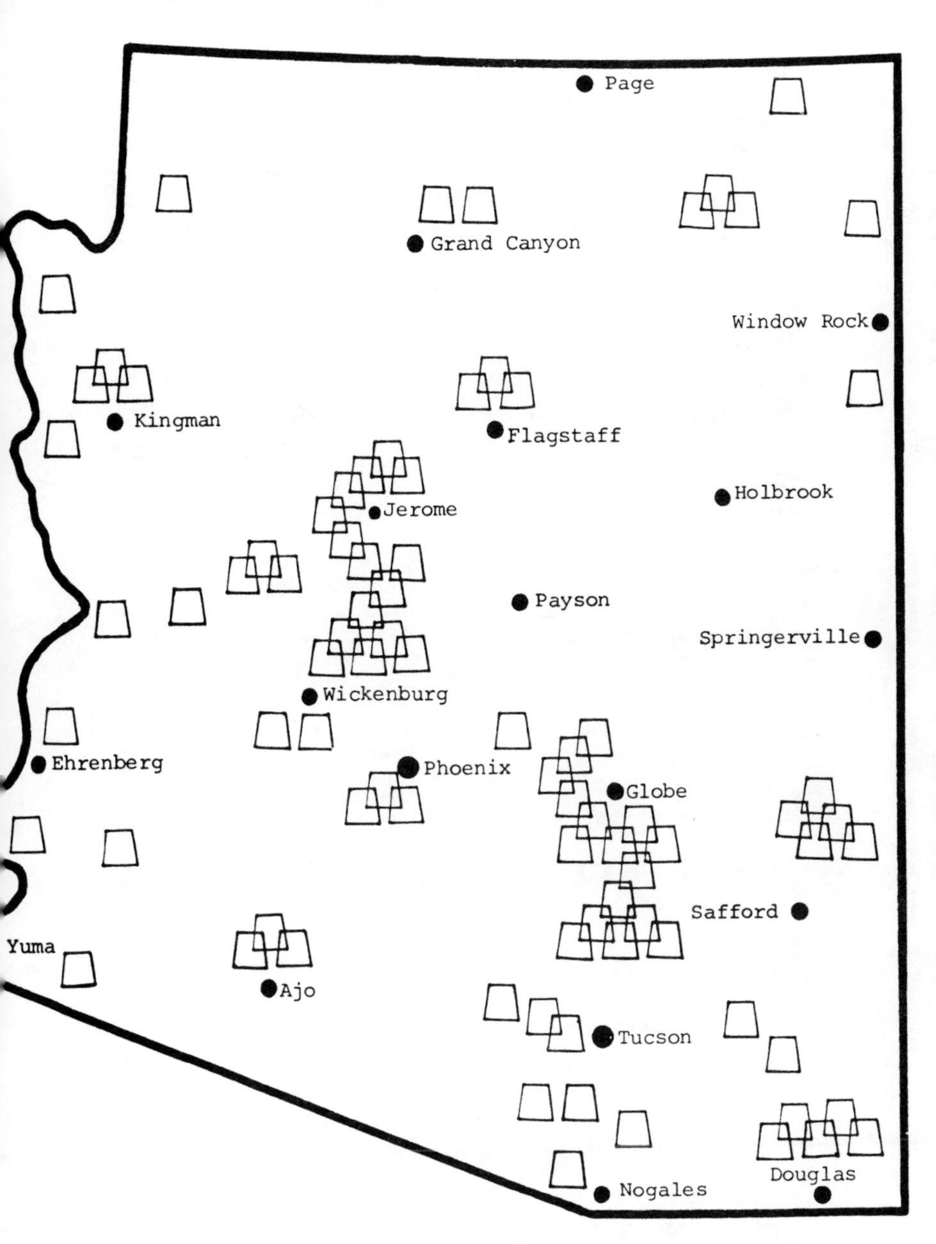

FIGURE 12. Principal mineral districts in Arizona. Each symbol represents $10,000,000 or more of minerals obtained from the area. (Adapted from Mardirosian, Charles A., MINING DISTRICTS AND MINERAL DEPOSITS OF ARIZONA. By permission.)

Mineral deposits (with the exception of coal and a few major copper areas) are mostly concentrated in the Mountain Province *(see Figure 12).* Symbols on the map indicate the approximate locations of principal mineral deposits that have produced at least $1 million (or many times that amount in a great number of cases). Most of the principal copper areas, for example, have produced more than $1 billion each in saleable products.

Most copper mined in Arizona now is low grade (one percent or less) obtained from open pit operations. Somewhat higher grade ore is obtained from a few underground mines. In either case, the ore is processed by either smelting or leaching. Sulfide ores ($CuFeS_2$, chalcopyrite; Cu_2S, chalcocite; $CuFeS_2$, Cu_5FeS_2, bornite) are concentrated and smelted in this manner:

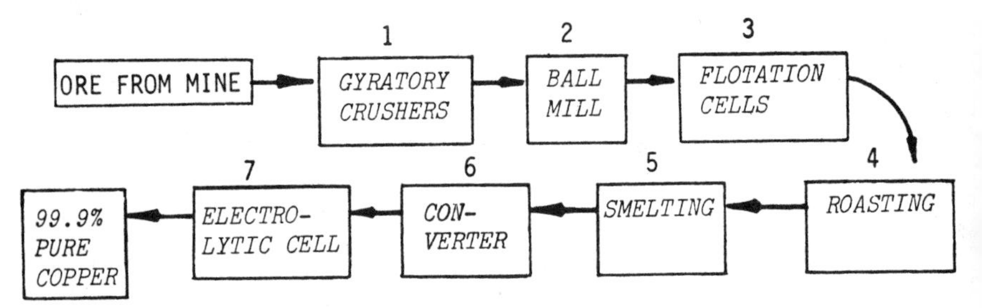

1. Ore from the mine is broken into pieces one-half-inch or less in size.

2. Steel balls in a large rotating drum grind the ore to powder.

3. Ore is mixed with water and a combination of soluble substances and the mixture is agitated strongly while air is forced into the tanks. The copper compounds adhere to the bubbles that form and float to the top and are removed. The worthless material falls to the bottom of the flotation cells and is removed to the tailings dump or pond. Molybdenum is also removed at this point. Gold, silver and other metals (mostly iron) remain with the copper.

4. Copper sulfides are changed to copper oxide and sulfur dioxide when heated to a high temperature in the presence of air: $2\,Cu_2S + 3\,O_2 \longrightarrow 2\,Cu_2O + 2\,SO_2\uparrow$. (Roasting may or may not be a part of the overall process at a given smelter.)

5. The smelter is charged with copper ore and lime and/or silica. The copper melts and becomes CuS while the iron and some other impurities combine with the lime and silica to form a glassy appearing slag which is removed and discarded. The product is copper matte containing 40-45 percent copper with the gold, silver, platinum and some iron not removed as part of the slag.

6. In the converter furnace, air is forced through the molten copper matte to which silica has been added. The remaining iron compounds combine with the silica and are removed as slag. $3\,CU_2S + 3\,O_2 \longrightarrow 6\,Cu + 3\,SO_2\uparrow$. The product is blister copper which is cast into anodes weighing several hundred pounds. Although the copper is now about 98 percent pure, it is not pure enough to be used for electrical conductors, the principal use for this metal.

7. Most anodes produced here are shipped out of the state (to areas closer to points of use) to refineries where it is electrolytically refined to 99.9 percent purity. Gold, silver and platinum are recovered in the refining process.

Oxygen ores of copper (Cu_2O, cuprite; CuO, melaconite; $CuCO_3 \cdot Cu(OH)_2$, malachite) are leached with sulfuric acid:

$$CuCO_3 \cdot Cu(OH)_2 + 2\,H_2SO_4 \longrightarrow$$
$$2\,CuSO_4 + 3\,H_2O + CO_2\uparrow$$

With the copper in solution as $CuSO_4$, iron is added to replace the copper from solution:

$$CuSO_4 + Fe \longrightarrow Cu\downarrow + FeSo_4.$$

The precipitated copper may then be melted and cast into anodes for refining. As part of air pollution control, some copper smelters are converting SO_2 gas from the flue gases to sulfuric acid which is then available for the leaching process:

$$2\,SO_2 + O_2 \longrightarrow 2\,SO_3 \qquad SO_3 + H_2O \longrightarrow H_2SO_4$$

Most open pit mines (Ajo, Morenci, Bisbee, Ray, etc.) have viewpoints from which one may observe the mining operation. Most of the copper companies do not provide for casual visits to concentrator plants or smelters but visits can be arranged to some of these on a group basis.

Chaparral Biotic Community

Due to the great range of elevations in the Mountain Province, we can find examples of most of the biotic communities *(see Figure 3).* In central Arizona the Chaparral and Pinyon-Juniper communities predominate, while in the southern areas of the province Desert Grassland and Oak Woodland communities are prevalent at the lower elevations.

Keep in mind that there are few, if any, sharp boundaries between any two communities. The Desert Shrub grades into Chaparral and that into Pinyon-Juniper and sometimes, because of local terrain conditions, one finds it difficult to make a decision. In addition, many plants found in the upper reaches of one zone also will be found in the lower elevations of the next. Thus there may be much duplication of plant types where adjacent biotic communities overlap.

Many people think that Chaparral is a species of plant. Actually, the word refers to a condition of the plant life generally. Any area where the dominant plant forms are low, brushy, shrubby and broadleaved can be called Chaparral, although the word is pretty much confined to use in the West. Some of the perennial plants that are common to the Chaparral life community are listed below.

Shrub Live Oak

Shrub-like trees that frequently form dense thickets. Small holly-like leaf with marginal spines. Fruit an edible acorn. Seldom more than 20 ft. tall.

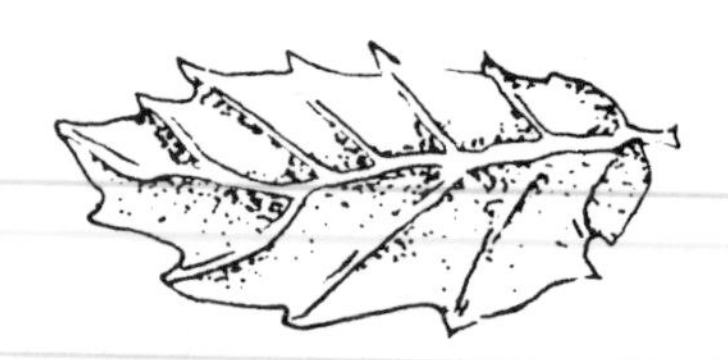

Squawbush (Skunkbush)

Shrub. Leaves have three leaflets that are deciduous and turn red in fall. Fruit is edible red berry.

Hackberry

Small tree about the same size and often growing with Shrub Oak. Leaves asymmetrical with rough surfaces that feel sticky to touch.

Hollygrape

Woody shrub with narrow, holly-like compound leaf (5 leaflets). Leaf spines are very sharp. Fruit is small blue berry.

Manzanita

Erect, oval, evergreen leaves. Smooth reddish bark is widely used for interior decoration. Frequently forms dense thickets. Fruit an edible berry.

Sotol (Spoon Plant)

Resembles the yuccas but the leaves do not have fibers peeling along edges. Tall flower stalk has club-like shape as small cream colored flowers cluster close together.

Agave (Century Plant)

Also resembles yuccas but leaves are thick, fleshy, with spines along margins and at tip. Flower stalk may grow 10-20 ft. tall within a few weeks. Flowers on horizontal branches are showy yellow-orange. Entire plant dies once seeds are mature.

Yucca, Catclaw, Jojoba, Pricklypear Cactus, Hedgehog Cactus

(See Desert Shrub Biotic Community Chapter)

Desertwillow

Not a willow. Does not grow in desert. Deciduous leaves long and narrow. Tree has a willow-like appearance except for showy, lavender flowers in Spring.

An Agave (Century Plant) in bloom. These plants are common in a wide elevation band in the Transition and Mountain provinces. This fast-growing flower stalk is about 20 feet tall. After the seeds mature, the entire plant dies.

A mixture of Chaparral and Piñon-Juniper vegetation. The low-growing Chaparral plants seen here frequently form dense thickets that sometimes make cowboys wish they were chuck-wagon cooks.

Pinyon-Juniper Biotic Community

This community is at a higher elevation, generally, than the Chaparral *(Figure 3).* Here the dominant trees are three Junipers and one Pine. Some of the Chaparral plants will be discovered here as well as some that occur more abundantly in the Ponderosa Pine community. A fifth tree that occurs here but is usually in the minority is the Arizona Cypress. The contrast between this and adjacent communities is quite pronounced and one has no difficulty in knowing when he has arrived in Pinyon-Juniper country.

Utah Juniper tree 20-25 feet tall and about the same width.

Utah Juniper

Junipers have tiny, scale-like leaves that overlap like shingles. The Utah Juniper is very common in this community. Trunk usually branches close to ground, giving the tree a somewhat globular shape. Rarely more than 25 to 30 ft. tall.

One-Seed Juniper

Less common and more tree-like than the Utah Juniper. May reach 50 ft. tall. Like all junipers, the fruit resembles a berry more than it does a cone.

Alligator Juniper

Also found in the Ponderosa Pine community to some extent. Trunks of older trees may be 10 feet or more in diameter although the height is seldom more than 30 to 40 ft. Bark fractures into square or rectangular plates resembling the skin of an alligator.

Pinyon Pine

Leaves needle-like, 1-2 in. long, attached singly to twig (Singleleaf Pinyon) or in bundles of two (Pinus edulis). These pines can be distinguished from the junipers by a glance at the leaves. Edible nuts are borne in a cone.

Pinyon Pine (Pinus edulis). This one is about 30 feet tall. Many people say the edible nut is not worth the trouble.

Cliffrose

Shrub or small tree may grow 20-25 feet tall but more commonly no more than head high. Leaves lobed and not more than 1 in. long. Showy flowers (white or cream) may cover the plant in spring or summer. Favorite browse of deer and livestock. Seeds have prominent whitish plumes.

Arizona Cypress

Tall conical tree superficially resembling the firs found at higher elevations. Leaves are quite similar to those of the junipers. The smooth, reddish bark detaches as large scales and strips.

Arizona Cypress 25 feet tall. Because of its shape, it is easily distinguished from the Pinyons and Junipers that occupy the same habitat.

Desert Grasslands and Oak Woodland Biotic Communities

These two communities intermix and alternate in the broad expanse of the Mountain Province in the southeastern part of the state *(Figure 2)* at elevations generally below the Pinyon-Juniper range. There are several native grasses or grass-like plants led by the Gramas, Lovegrass and Fescue. Most grassland areas are not entirely grass, and scattered stands of Yuccas, Cholla cacti, Junipers and evergreen Oaks are seen.

Oak woodland occurs in small areas of relatively dense stands of evergreen Oaks and more often as dispersed patches of trees in predominantly grasslands areas. The principal oak in southeastern Arizona is the Emory Oak, also called Black Oak or Blackjack. The tree grows to about 50 ft. tall. Other evergreen oaks in this community include the Arizona Oak, Canyon Live Oak and Mexican Blue Oak.

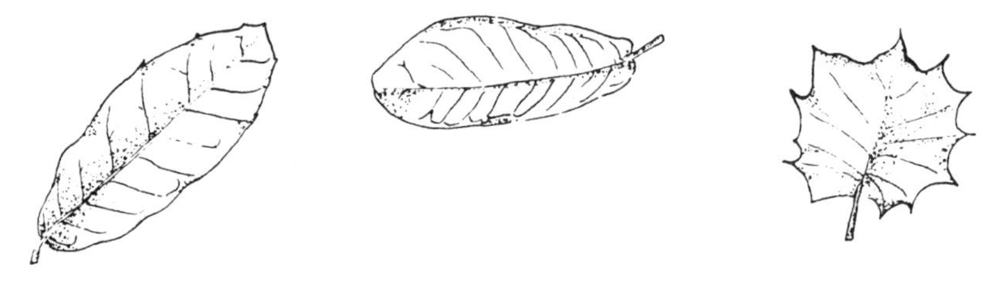

Animal Life

Animal life in the Chaparral, Pinyon-Juniper, Oak Woodland and Desert Grasslands communities differs a great deal from that of the Desert Shrub region. More cover, more water and lower temperatures bring about certain modifications in the numbers and kinds of animals we would find if we were to compare a square mile of this habitat with an equal area of the Desert Shrub ecosystem.

There would be, for example, an increase in the number of browsing and grazing animals—especially Deer and Antelope that prefer the leaves of shrubs and grasses for food. This results in an increase in the predators that depend upon these animals. Mountain Lions in particular could be expected to be more numerous.

BOBCAT

MOUNTAIN LION

More animals that prefer to live far from man's habitats will be found in the Mountain Province region. The Black Bear that occupies some higher elevations in the province is a good example. Bobcats, Eagles, Turkeys, and Tree and Rock Squirrels are a few other people-shy animals inhabiting the area.

Many of the Desert Shrub birds also are found in these communities. In addition, one may observe: Arizona Jay, Bluebird, Junco, Sparrows (especially White Crowned), Band-tailed Pigeon, Hawks, Ravens, Mearns Quail, Gambel Quail, Towhee, and a number of Warblers and Nuthatches.

GAMBEL'S QUAIL

RED-TAILED HAWK

Animals listed for the Desert Shrub community that would not be found here or only rarely are: Roadrunner, Gila Woodpecker, Cactus Wren, Prairie Dog, Kangaroo Rat, Sonora Whitetail Deer, Swifts, Geckos, Whiptails, Gila Monster, Sidewinder Rattlesnake, Colorado River Toad, Desert Tortoise, Chuckwalla.

The permanent streams, lakes, tanks and rivers of these communities harbor a variety of aquatic animals that depend either directly or indirectly upon water plants (chiefly algae), insects and microscopic animals that form the first links in the fresh water food chains and webs. Warm water game fish include Large-mouth Bass, Crappie, Bluegill, Catfish, Striped Bass and Pike.

At higher elevations, one may find several species of Trout. The Rainbow trout is the most common, since it is the species most often planted for the benefit of fishermen. German Brown, Eastern Brook and Arizona Native trout are to be found in certain streams in the provinces.

#3 Transition Province

Although this province is the smallest in area, it is one of the most varied and interesting and plays host to more summer visitors than any comparable area in the state.

Generally, it lies between the rugged jumble of the Mountain area and the escarpment (The Rim) that is the exposed southern edge of the Colorado Plateau *(Figures 2 and 7).* The area includes the zone of contact between the igneous and metamorphic complex of the Mountain province and the sedimentary layers of the Plateau.

Most of the surface area formations are the limestones, sandstones, conglomerates and shales (Appendix B) making up the lower layers of the Plateau *(Figure 7)* that have been exposed by the erosive action of the headwaters of the river systems removing the overlying layers. When viewed from a distance or from the air, the appearance of the area is that of a wooded, relatively level inter-montane basin. Closer inspection, however, reveals that much of the province is quite rugged. Low mountains and steep-walled canyons are frequent geomorphic features.

The Rim (called the Mogollon Rim in central Arizona) is the result of the headward erosion of the streams of the province. Softer layers of rock in the lower part of the Plateau formations are continually being removed, while the more resistant upper layers break off and tumble down under the influence of gravity. Although the Rim, when viewed from a distance, appears to be smooth and straight, it is in reality very irregular *(Figure 13).* The Rim was not formed by a gigantic fault or break in the earth's crust—despite the belief of many people.

Some of the limestones of the region are of the lower and middle Paleozoic (formed 300 to 400 million years ago) and contain abundant fossils of animals that lived in shallow seas that covered this section of the Southwest at that time. Some of the more common fossils to be found are:

Brachiopods

Also called Lamp Shells. Bivalve (clam or oyster type animal belonging to the phylum Brachiopoda) having the two shells of unequal size. There are more than 25,000 fossil species of which only a few kinds are found in this area.

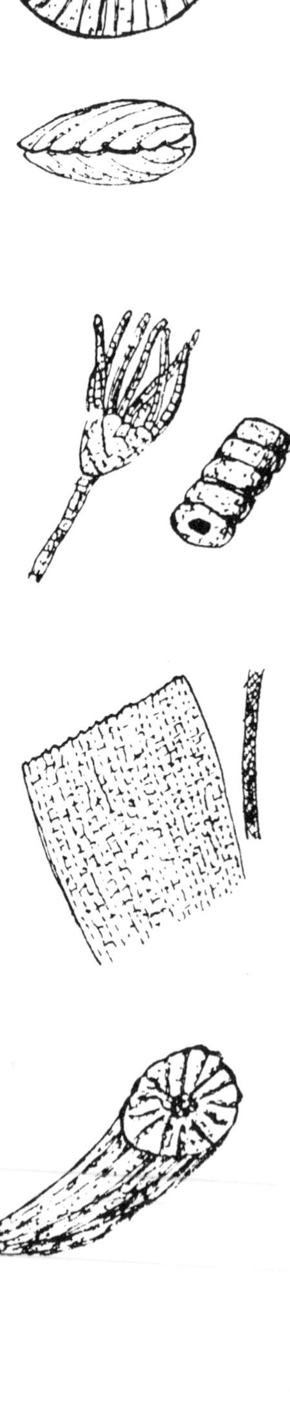

Crinoids

Also called Sea Lilies because of their resemblance to flowers. They were, however, true animals of the phylum Echinodermata. Most of the fossils are parts of the segmented stems or tentacles. Modern forms include the Starfishes, Sea Urchins and Sea Lilies.

Bryozoans

Also called Moss Animals. Branching, colonial animals easily mistaken for sea weed or coral. Fossils are fern-like grids and very small stems somewhat resembling, on a tiny scale, the woody skeletons of some species of Cholla cacti.

Horn Coral

A general common name for a group of fossil corals that grew in colonies. Each individual resembles a short, inverted cow's horn. These fossils are not as numerous in the area as are the other three types.

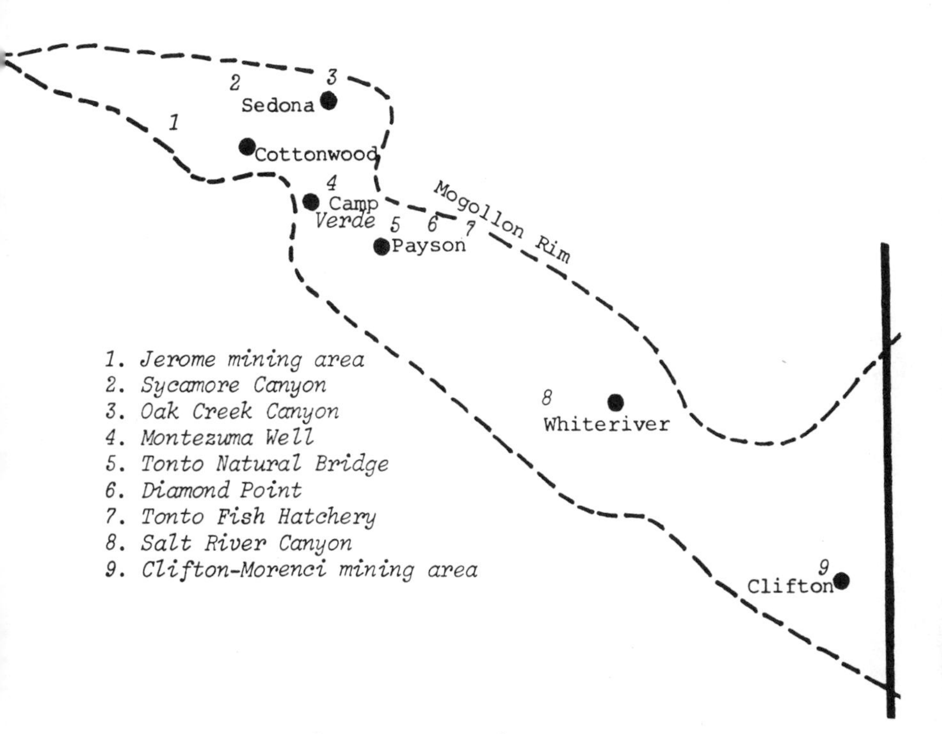

FIGURE 13a. The Transition Physiographic Province.

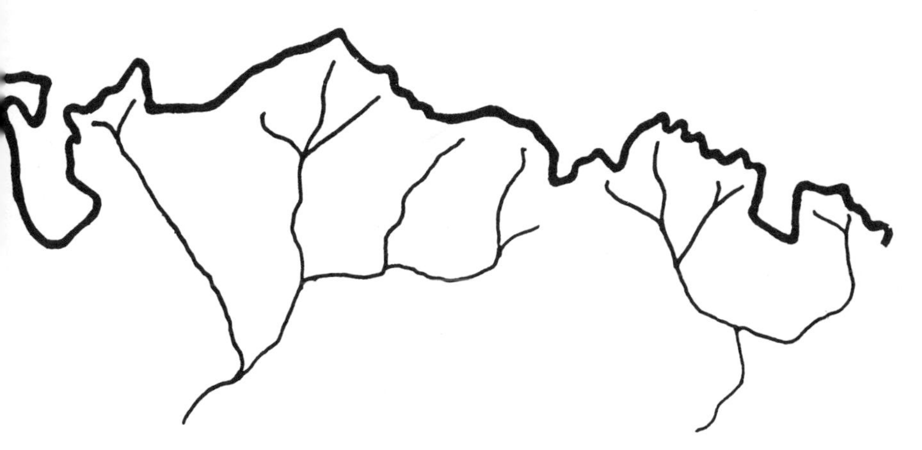

FIGURE 13b. A portion of the Mogollon Rim in central Arizona extending from the vicinity of Pine to Christopher Creek. The upper East Verde River and Tonto Creek drainages are shown.

Tonto Natural Bridge near Payson is so huge that photographs seldom do it justice. This portion of the east wall beneath the bridge dwarfs the person standing to the right and a little below center of photo.

Other Geologic Features

DIAMOND POINT

This prominent ridge east of Payson is part of the Colorado Plateau that was separated by the removal of material between it and the Mogollon Rim by the erosive action of Tonto Creek and the East Verde River.

The mountain consists mostly of layers of limestone lying almost horizontal. It gets its name from the abundance of quartz crystals that have weathered out of the limestone. These crystals, which superficially resemble cut diamonds, seem to have precipitated from ground water in cavities in the limestone during its formation. The quartz is much more resistant to weathering than is the surrounding limestone and is left behind when the limestone is dissolved by rain and groundwater containing a slight amount of carbonic acid (H_2CO_3).

Many limestone sinks (sinkholes) are located on the flanks of the ridge and at least one small limestone cavern is known. Calcite, the form that calcium carbonate (Appendix B) takes when it precipitates in large cavities underground, is found on the surface; an indication that caverns probably also were located above the present ground surface in the past. Specimens of hematite, a form of iron oxide, also are found on the surface.

The Forest Service tower on the summit of Diamond Point is at about 6500 feet elevation and is manned only during the fire season—approximately May until October.

TONTO NATURAL BRIDGE

A unique geologic feature of the province is the travertine natural bridge located about three miles west of the highway between Payson and Pine.

This structure was (and continues to be) formed by the deposition of calcium carbonate (travertine) from the waters of several natural springs in the east wall of the

Montezuma's Castle is not a castle and was never seen by Montezuma. Prehistoric Sinagua Indians found the eroded Verde Lake limestone along Beaver Creek a convenient building site.

Montezuma's Well. A large spring that dissolved the overlying layers of Verde Lake limestone.

canyon of Pine Creek. While the travertine is being deposited to form the upper portion of the bridge, Pine Creek prevents deposition in the lower parts. The rock making up the canyon walls is dense, crystalline quartzite and rhyolite, mostly red or pinkish and contrasts sharply with the gray-white, relatively soft travertine of the bridge itself.

No one can know for certain how long nature has been building this formation. The dimensions, however, should convince anyone that it was not an overnight job: height of bridge, 183 ft.; length of tunnel, 400 ft., width of tunnel, 150 ft. Compare these measurements with the 300 ft. length of a football field.

INTERMONTANE BASINS

The most notable feature of the Transition Province is the series of unconnected broad valleys generated by the erosion and deposition of the province's drainage systems. From northwest to southeast the more prominent of these valleys are: Chino Valley, Verde Valley, Tonto Basin and the Gila River Valley east of Globe. All of these are locally important agricultural areas.

An interesting sedimentary formation in the Verde Valley is the distinctive soft, white limestone that was deposited in a large lake in late Pliocene time. The lake formed as the result of a lava flow that dammed the Verde River south of where Camp Verde is now located. The lake was about 15 miles wide by 35 miles long. In time, the river eroded the lava dam and the limestone deposits became the present ground surface. Both Montezuma's Castle and Well are in the Verde Lake limestone.

SEDONA RED ROCKS AREA

The beautifully carved red and buff sandstones of the Sedona, Oak Creek and Sycamore Canyon region are some of the same formations exposed in Grand Canyon almost 100 miles to the north. The Coconino sandstone (Permian) forms the white to buff upper portions of this highly dissected area, while the Supai sandstone (Pennsylvanian) is the striking red layers lower down.

Oak Creek Canyon resulted from a large north-south fault through the plateau formations and the subsequent erosion by Oak Creek through the broken and weakened zone. The fault is easily seen from the developed view point on the edge of the rim at the head of the canyon. Something to note is that the distinctive sandstone formations are well developed only where the protective basaltic cap rock is missing.

Colorful escarpments in the Sedona area form the southern edge of the Colorado Plateau for some 40 miles.

National Forests

Most of the Transition and Mountain provinces and limited areas of the Colorado Plateau and Basin and Range provinces are U.S. National Forest lands managed by the Forest Service, a division of the U.S. Department of Agriculture.

The Forest Service subscribes to the philosophy of multiple use and sustained yield in its management of your national forests. Conservation here means making the wisest use of the natural resources of the forests without permanently impairing their ability to keep producing.

The Forest Service is concerned with five areas under which multiple use and sustained yield concepts operate successfully:

Water

Uncontrolled cutting and burning of the forests results in excessive runoff of surface water that causes flooding of the rivers and silting of reservoirs.

Watershed management in the Tonto National Forest is of particular importance because of Salt River Project dams on the Salt and Verde rivers. Tonto Forest was established to protect a major portion of this watershed and this accounts for the fact that the greatest part of the 2,900,000 acres are desert or chaparral land that produce no marketable timber.

Timber

The higher elevations of the forests produce high grade construction timber. Ponderosa pine is by far the principal sawlog species, although significant amounts of White and Douglas Fir are harvested. The Forest Service selects and sells standing trees to logging contractors who remove the trees, in the form of sawlogs, to the mills in the area.

Visitors to a sawmill see the logs moved through the mill pond (if there is one) to the large band-saws where the initial sawing of the log takes place. Large boards coming from the band-saw may be cut to lesser thicknesses by circular or band saws farther along the line. Most of the rough-sawed lumber is taken to the planing mill for final smoothing, grading and sizing. Some of the lumber is dipped in a preservative solution before being strapped into bundles for shipment to builders and building supply firms.

Minor uses for timber from the forests are pulpwood (primarily for the pulp mill at Snowflake), poles, posts, manzanita for decoration, and Christmas trees. Bark,

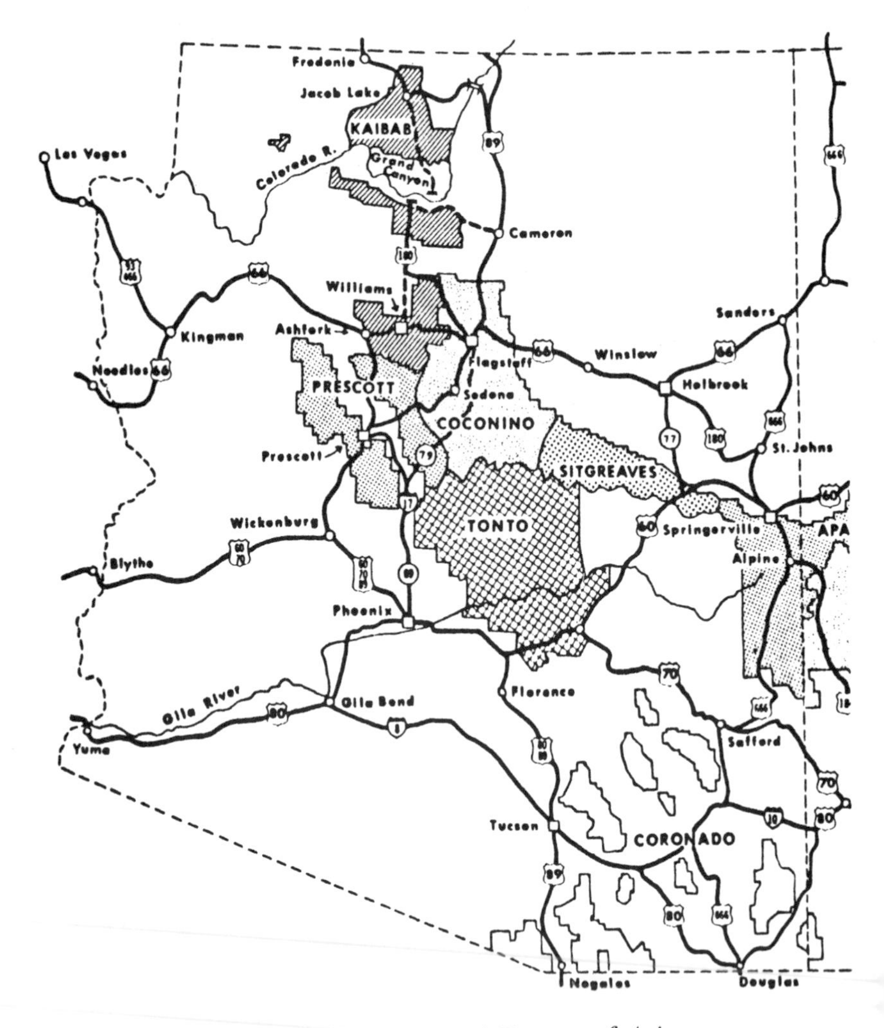

FIGURE 14. The National Forests of Arizona.

slabs, scraps, shavings and sawdust may be burned to supply heat to drying kilns or to make steam to generate electricity. Otherwise, the bark and sawdust can be converted to mulch and the slabs chipped for use in manufacturing paper and particle board.

Grazing

Many thousands of cattle and sheep graze on the national forests. Ranchers have grazing allotments and pay a certain amount per animal for the grazing privilege. Constantly changing conditions that affect the amount of available food require close cooperation between the Forest Service rangers and the ranchers to permit maximum utilization of the range without causing permanent damage to this resource.

Wildlife

The Forest Service maintains the habitats for wildlife in the forests under its jurisdiction but has very little to do with the regulation of hunting and fishing, since this is the province of the Arizona Game and Fish Department. The two agencies cooperate in attempting to maintain a balance between the production and harvesting of the many game animals inhabiting the forests.

Recreation

Each year the national forests in Arizona are visited by several million people seeking escape from the heat and hurry of metropolitan areas at lower elevations. The Forest Service has built and maintains many picnic and camp grounds throughout the region—including several along the Salt River and its lakes in the desert community.

Of all the problems faced by the Forest Service, man is by far the most vexing. Thoughtless littering, vandalism and carelessness with fire result in the expenditure of much money and many man-hours by our forest rangers that easily could be put to much better use.

Ponderosa Pine and Pine-Fir Biotic Communities

Although there are large areas of Chaparral, Pinyon-Juniper, and Desert Grassland in the Transition province, the communities that summer visitors are seeking are the big trees of the Ponderosa Pine and Pine-Fir communities. Thoughts of these trees generate visions of cool crisp air, clear trout streams and lazy vacation days.

The Pine-Fir community is dominated by a mixture of mostly Ponderosa pines and Douglas and White firs, whereas the Ponderosa community is noted for the abundance of Ponderosa pine that is the only very large tree in most areas.

Principal trees and shrubs in the two communities are:

Ponderosa Pine

(Western Yellow Pine) Needles 5 to 10 in. long. Attached to twig in bundles of three. Bark rough and dark on young trees; orangish, smoother on older trees. Principal timber tree of the Southwest. Large specimens may exceed 150 ft. and be four feet or more through at the base.

Limber Pine

Much smaller tree than Ponderosa. Not numerous. Needles 1 to 4 in. long in bundles of four or five. Young branches can be tied in a knot.

Ponderosa pines on the Colorado Plateau. Largest tree is more than 100 feet tall. Smaller trees in foreground called "Blackjack" by many people.

Arizona Pine

Also called Apache pine. Smaller than Ponderosa. Long needles (9 to 15 in.) three or four in bundle. Found mostly in southeastern Arizona above 5000 ft. Not common.

White Fir

Large evergreen tree. Needles short, flat, attached singly to twig and usually grow horizontally from opposite sides. Conical shape of tree and bluish cast of needles cause frequent confusion with Colorado Blue Spruce which is seldom seen at these elevations. Cone is smooth without bracts or spines.

Douglas Fir

Needles generally smaller than White Fir. Needles grow all around the twig. Cone has 3-lobed, papery protruding bracts.

Subalpine Fir

Similar to White Fir except that needles curve sharply upward after starting horizontally from twig. Not as common as White Fir in these communities.

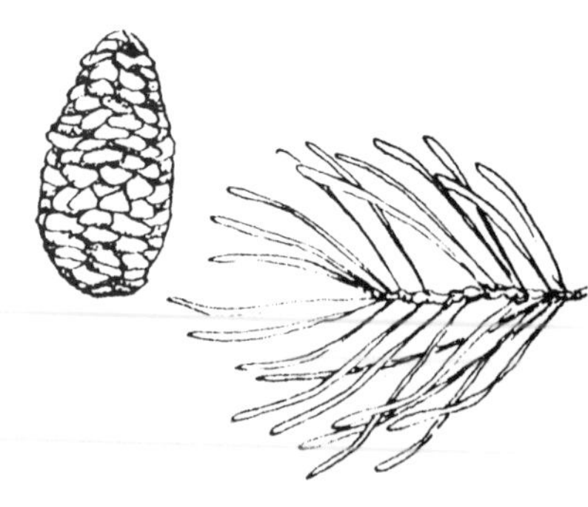

The Douglas fir is a large evergreen tree found growing among Ponderosa pines in scattered areas of the Transition and Colorado Plateau provinces.

Gambel Oak

Leaves lobed, rounded, turn brown and drop in fall. Tree usually no more than about 30 ft. tall. Bark rough and gray. Fruit an acorn.

Arizona White Oak

Sometimes called Arizona Live Oak. Evergreen. Leaves may take several forms on same tree; usually holly-like or oval with rough margins. Fruit an acorn.

Maples

(Bigtooth, Dwarf and Rocky Mountain) All are small trees. Leaves opposite, lobed with toothed margins. Leaves turn bright yellow or scarlet in fall. Fruit a winged seed.

Alligator Juniper

Utah Juniper

One-Seed Juniper

(See Pinyon-Juniper Community)

Southwestern Locust

Small tree with compound leaves 8 to 12 in. long. Showy flowers are pinkish or lavender in large pendant clusters. Commonly forms thickets.

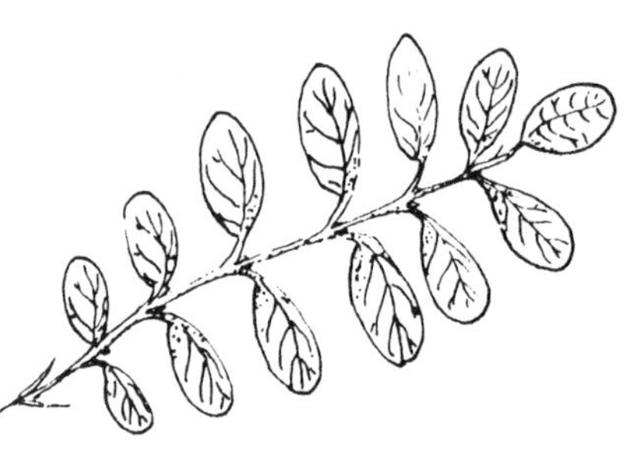

Manzanita

(See Chaparral Community)

Arizona White oak. An evergreen oak found extensively in the Transition province. Much smaller than the Eastern Woodlands oaks, this mature tree is only about 30 feet tall.

Wild Cherry

Also called Bitter Cherry. Small tree (20 feet or so). Small bitter fruit, mostly seed. Bark smooth, papery; distinctive wild cherry odor when scraped.

Sugar Sumac

Also Sugarbush. Shrub with evergreen leaves 2 or 3 in. long. General appearance similar to Manzanita but bark is not red.

Poison Ivy

Grows as low shrub or vine. Leaves compound; three leaflets two or more inches long. Shiny green upper surfaces turn red in fall. Fruit a small white berry. Toxic oil in all parts of plant causes severe skin irritation in allergic individuals.

(Space does not permit the listing of the many more shrubs, grasses and annuals that make up the understory of the forest. In addition, one may find an abundance of lichens, mosses, ferns, saprophytes and parasites. The reader is again referred to Appendix A for sources of additional information.)

Animal Life

The increased elevations and resulting temperature decrease, moisture increase and a different vegetative cover causes some changes in the numbers and kinds of animals in these communities when compared with other biotic communities at lower elevations.

The abundance of cone and nut bearing trees allows an expected increase in animals who depend upon these foods. Squirrels, for example, are very common in the Pine-Fir forests. The Arizona Gray squirrel is seen much more often than the larger Tassel-Eared or Abert's squirrel. The Gray-Necked and Cliff chipmunks also depend heavily upon the big tree fruits.

Since one of the favorite foods of the Porcupine is the bark of young conifer trees, we would expect to find more of these animals here, although they are not plentiful and are seldom seen.

STRIPED SKUNK

SPOTTED SKUNK

Other mammals that are found in greater numbers in these communities are Skunks (Spotted and Striped), Red Foxes, Beaver (now rare in most of Arizona) and Black Bear.

The Transition province is home for many Mule deer and some White-Tailed deer. During summer, the deer from lower elevations will move upward and during mid-winter, deer (and sometimes Elk) will move into this area from the higher elevations. And, of course, their chief enemy, the Mountain Lion, may follow along. The Mountain Lion is one of the most widely distributed and least known animals of the Southwest. Because of its stealthy, retiring nature, few casual visitors to its home areas have observed it in the wild. Attacks upon humans by this animal are almost unknown.

Some of the Transition region animals hibernate for short periods during the coldest part of the winter. This adaptation is not as widespread or as vital here as at higher elevations or in more northerly latitudes.

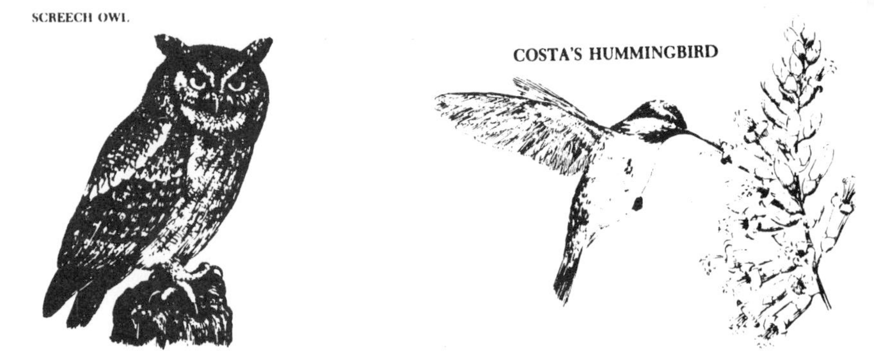
SCREECH OWL
COSTA'S HUMMINGBIRD

This is the habitat of the Wild Turkey. Their tracks may be found along the streams and their calls are heard breaking the stillness of the forest. Some other birds observed in these high forests are Screech Owls, Hummingbirds, Juncos, Flycatchers, Whippoorwills, Hermit Thrush, Western Tanager, Blue Grouse, Evening Grosbeak and Steller's Jay. The Dipper or Water Ouzel can be seen along streams as it dips into the water after aquatic insects or their larvae.

WESTERN DIAMONDBACK RATTLESNAKE
WESTERN HOGNOSE SNAKE

A number of harmless snakes, as well as the poisonous Western Diamondback Rattlesnake, have their homes here: Gopher Snake (Bull Snake), Blue Racer, Garter Snake and the Hognosed Snake who, by the way, frequently is accused of being a rattler because of its coloration and the shape of its head. Another case of mistaken identity is the harmless Mountain King Snake and the highly poisonous Sonoran Coral Snake. Both are brightly colored with red, black and yellow bands around the body—but the Coral Snake is found only at the lower desert elevations.

TONTO FISH HATCHERY

This installation is an example of the several state and federal hatcheries in the state. The Tonto hatchery is operated by the Arizona Game and Fish Department and is located about four miles north of Kohl's Ranch which is some 17 miles east of Payson on Arizona 260. Visitors are welcome and no prior arrangements are necessary. The primary function of this hatchery is to raise and "plant" trout in the streams and lakes in the mountainous parts of the state.

Trout eggs, imported from commercial sources in some of the eastern states, are hatched in tiers of trays in the main hatchery building. About 1,000,000 eggs comprise a hatch, although several million fish in various stages of development are in the hatchery at any given time. Water at about 55 degrees F. from the spring that is the source of Tonto Creek circulates over the eggs during hatching.

Newly hatched trout called "fry" are kept in troughs in the hatchery house for several weeks before being transferred to the rectangular concrete tanks outside. When the small fish reach a length of several inches, they are moved to the large rearing ponds where they remain until ready to plant.

It takes approximately 18 months to raise a Rainbow Trout to the plantable size of 9 to 12 inches long. The entire process is paid for by revenues realized from the sale of state licenses to fishermen.

As the trout grow larger, the size of food pellets is increased proportionately. This food is a formulation designed to produce large, healthy fish in a minimum of time. A check of the label on a feed sack in the hatchery house will reveal that most fish (and many people) never had it so good!

The trout finally are hauled in tank trucks to the streams and lakes in the area during the heavy fishing period from May until September. The practice of planting trout in this manner is frequently referred to as "put and take" fishing.

#4 Colorado Plateau Province

This province occupies about one-third of the state and continues into Utah to the north and New Mexico and Colorado to the east and northeast. Physiographically, the province resembles a gigantic stone layer cake with some serious blemishes. The Colorado River and its tributaries have cut some massive gashes into the northern portion where the Grand Canyon exposes nearly a vertical mile of almost horizontal rock layers. In the southern part (principally the Flagstaff and White Mountain areas) the cake is topped with some jumbled dark frosting in the form of ancient and recent volcanic eruptions *(Figure 7).*

The surface of the plateau consists of basaltic lavas in the southern portion and the upper layers of sedimentary lime-

Grand Canyon displays about one billion years of geologic history. Figures 11 and 15 correlate the sedimentary and metamorphic formations with geologic time.

Sunset Crater northeast of Flagstaff is an example of recent volcanism. The eruption that built the crater took place in 1054—less than 1,000 years ago.

stones, shales and sandstones in the central and northern areas here listed in order of decreasing age of deposition and from lower to upper layers as one proceeds generally toward the northeastern corner of the state: Coconino, Kaibab and de Chelly sandstones (Permian); Chinle and Moenkopi silts and shales (Triassic); Kayenta and Navajo sandstones (Triassic); Cow Springs sandstone and Morrison Formation sandstone, mudstone, shale (Jurassic); Mancos shale, Dakota sandstone and Mesa Verde Group sandstones (Cretaceous). The Seligman-Williams-Flagstaff and Show Low-McNary-Springerville volcanics are easily distinguishable from the underlying and adjacent plateau sedimentaries.

Grand Canyon is, of course, the showcase of the plateau country in exhibiting about a billion years of earth history *(Figure 15)*. The record is incomplete and there are many breaks (unconformities) indicating long lapses of time between the deposition of present seemingly successive layers. Indeed, to present an unbroken record of those one billion years, the canyon would have to be about 180 miles deep!

The Colorado River system has been carving the canyon country for only 15 to 20 million years—a relative instant as geologic time is reckoned. In the Grand Canyon, the river is about 2500 feet above sea level and probably has been at about the same level since it took its present course. Geologists say that the rate at which the river has been cutting down through the plateau rocks is about equal to the rate at which the whole area has been (and still is being) elevated above sea level by gigantic forces within the earth

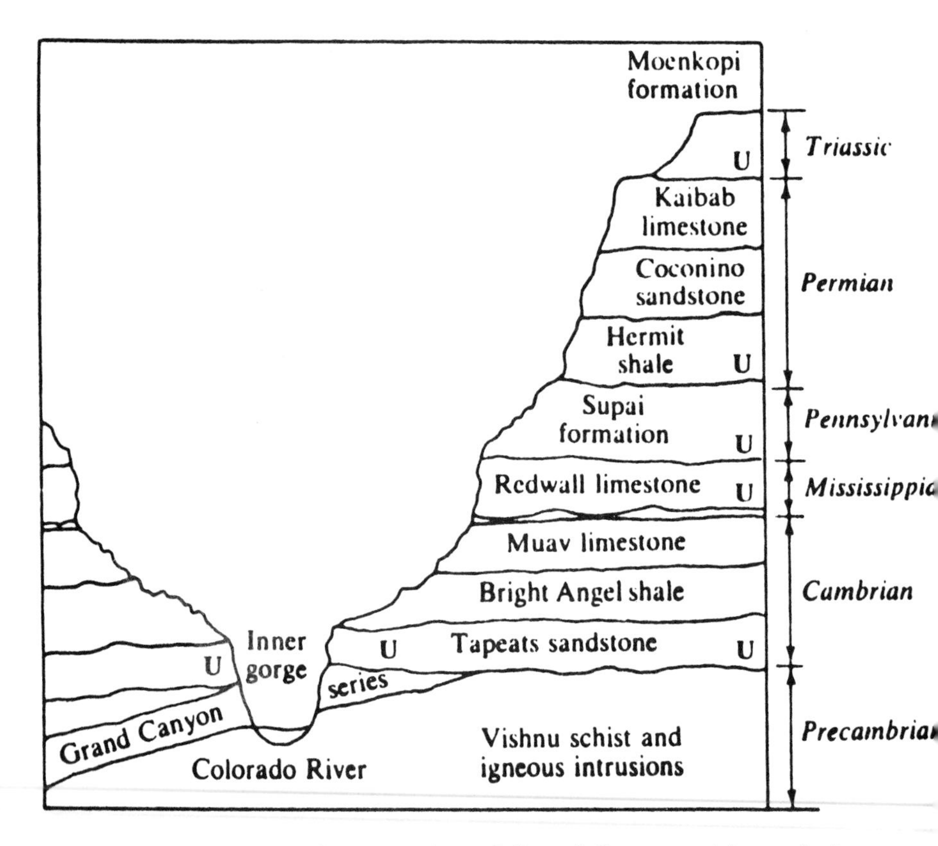

FIGURE 15. Cross section of Grand Canyon with south rim on right. Major unconformities are labeled U.

San Francisco Peaks near Flagstaff. Reaching an elevation of more than 12,000 feet, these mountains are the result of the buildup of volcanic material that broke through sedimentary layers of the Colorado Plateau.

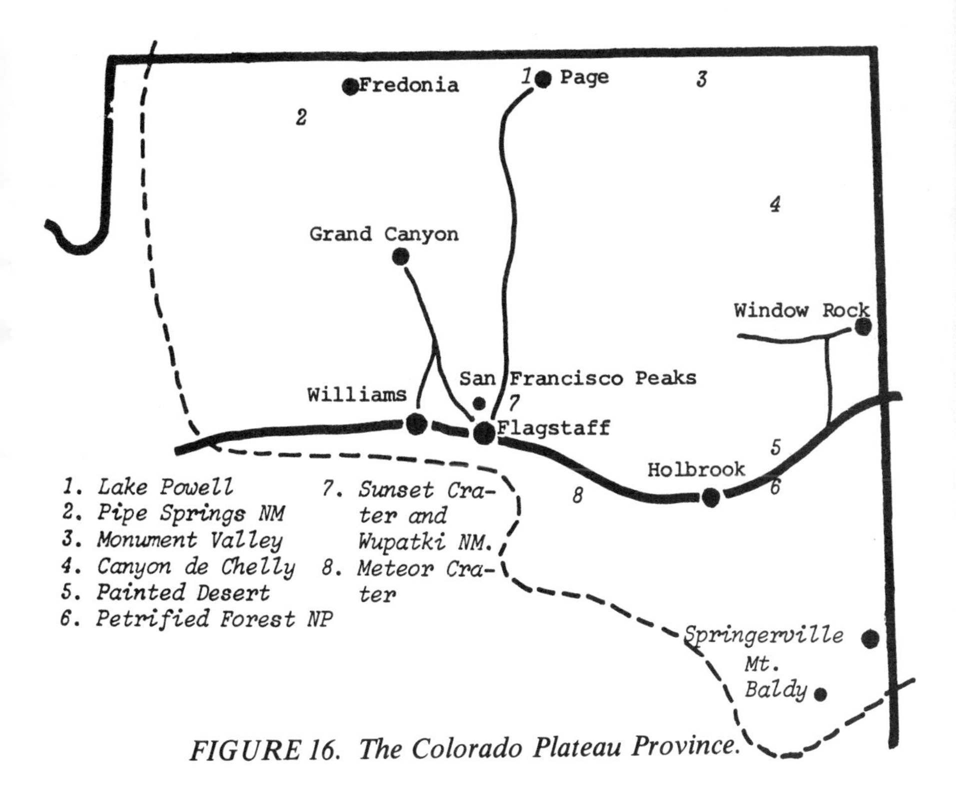

FIGURE 16. The Colorado Plateau Province.

Biotic Communities

Due (again) to the great range in elevation (2000 feet along the Colorado River in the northwestern corner of the state to more than 12,600 feet at the summit of the San Francisco Peaks), almost all of the biotic communities are represented. Perhaps the best known is the Ponderosa Pine community that extends in a wide band across the Plateau from near the northern border of the state southward to the Rim and into the Transition province in many places.

Intermingled with the Ponderosa Pine community are areas of Pine-Fir, Spruce-Fir-Aspen and Riparian Woodland depending upon elevations in the Kaibab Plateau north of Grand Canyon, the mountains in the Flagstaff area, and the White Mountains in the east-central part of the state.

California's Mohave Desert biotic community occupies portions of the Basin and Range, Mountain and Colorado Plateau provinces in the northwestern corner of Arizona. The dominant plant here is Creosotebush but the eye-catching plants are the tree-like Mohave Yucca and the Joshua Tree which is also a member of the yucca group. These plants in Arizona are restricted to a narrow band adjacent to the western border north of Parker and Wickenburg.

To the west, east and northeast of the Ponderosa Pine belt lie vast areas of Desert Grasslands and Sagebrush Desert (Mohave Desert type vegetation). The dominant plants are grasses (where overgrazing has not completely removed them) and several sages: Big Sagebrush, Black Sagebrush and Sand Sagebrush. Other prominent plants are Greasewood and Pricklypear cactus. A few other cacti typical of the Desert Shrub community sometimes are found but seldom in abundance.

Spruce-Fir-Aspen Biotic Community

This community generally lies above the Ponderosa and Pine-Fir communities but, as usual, variations caused by local conditions are common. The Spruce-Fir-Aspen association is the highest elevation at which are found what we consider normal size trees. Above this zone is the Alpine Tundra with its grasses, herbaceous flowering plants, dwarfed Engelmann spruce, Bristlecone pines and dwarf junipers.

Engelmann Spruce

Tall tree common above 8000 feet. Needles four-sided, about one in. long. Cones small with scales. Limbs may droop somewhat and lower ones almost touch the ground.

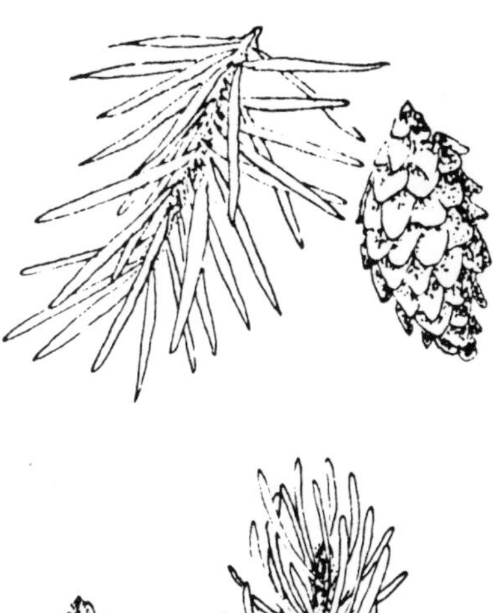

Colorado Blue Spruce

Seldom found below 8500 feet in Arizona. Tall, stately, conical tree with limbs at right angles from trunk. Needles four-sided, about one in. long with definite bluish cast. White Fir resembles this tree at a distance but details are quite distinctive.

Quaking Aspen

Tall straight trunk with smooth white bark. Small leaves, rounded at base with finely toothed margin. Not common below about 7000 feet. Favorite beaver food and dam building material.

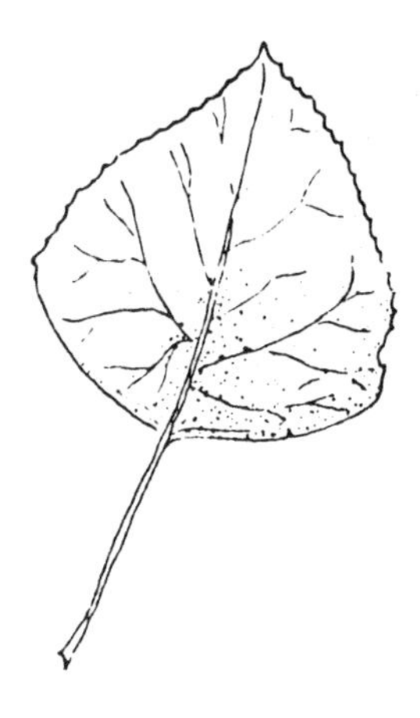

White Fir
Subalpine Fir
Douglas Fir
Maples

(See Ponderosa Pine and Pine-Fir Communities)

ANIMAL LIFE

In addition to most of the animals already listed for the higher elevation communities, animals inhabiting the Spruce-Fir-Aspen areas are: This is the summer range of the largest of all southwestern deer, the Elk. The larger Merriam's Elk that was native to the area was exterminated 100 years ago and the present species is the Wyoming Elk. These animals sometimes can be seen near dusk grazing in the open meadows of the high forests in summer. The Bighorn mountain sheep inhabits some areas in this community but is rarely seen. Other animals not already mentioned include Prairie Dogs, Kaibab Squirrels, Porcupines and Buffalo. The Buffalo are state owned and confined to a fenced range in Houserock Valley north of the Colorado River.

BIGHORN

Riparian Woodland Biotic Community

In some areas this community is designated "Canyon Hardwoods" by the U.S. Forest Service. The Riparian community is found cutting across every other biotic association except the Spruce-Fir-Aspen and Alpine Tundra. The community is the narrow band of plants that grow close to and are dependent upon flowing water in streams and rivers or places where water is close to the soil surface in washes and usually dry stream beds.

The community is apparent along the bottom of almost every canyon in the state but is also found along streams and washes in the Transition and Basin and Range provinces where the watercourses have not carved deep canyons. Principal trees of the Riparian Woodland are:

Cottonwood

(See Desert Shrub Community)

Mesquite

(See Desert Shrub Community)

Tamarisk

(Salt-cedar) Native of Mediterranean region accidentally introduced into the Southwest. Small tree that resembles junipers but is not evergreen. Small, scale-like leaves turn yellow in Fall. Forms thickets along permanent watercourses. Mostly a nuisance type plant.

Willow

Trees of various sizes. Bark rough and loose on older trees. Leaves are characteristically long and narrow.

Sycamore trees in winter on flooding Dry Beaver Creek. Note white bark and irregular shape. Not to be confused with white bark Aspen trees found only at much higher elevation.

Sycamore

Large tree frequently found growing along watercourses with Cottonwood. Bark smooth, light brown or green to white. Leaves large, five-lobed. Fruit a ball 1 to 1½ in. diameter.

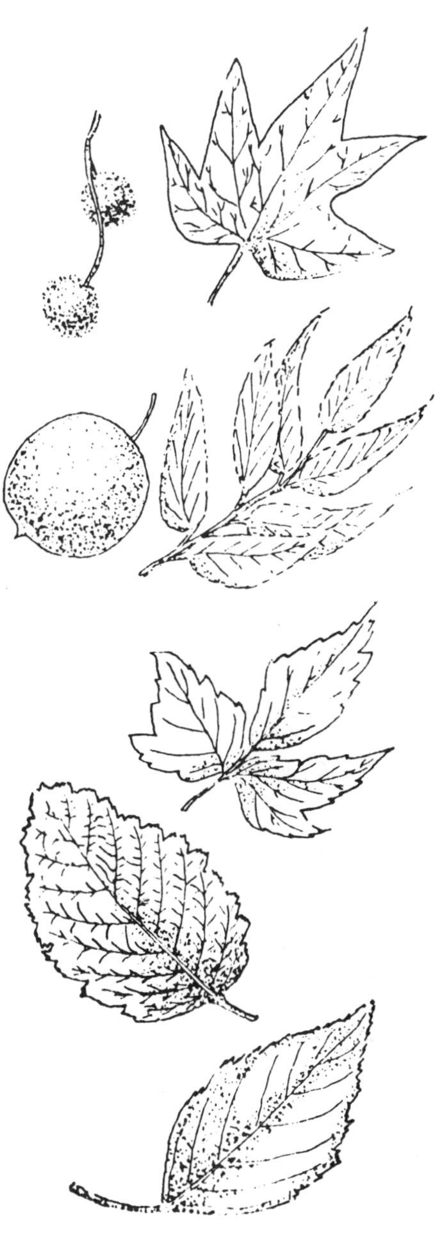

Arizona Walnut

Small to medium size trees with long, compound leaf. Margins of leaves are toothed. Nuts are smooth, one in. or less in diameter.

Box Elder

Generally resembles Maples but leaves are compound with three leaflets. Often confused with Poison Ivy which grows as a vine or shrub, not a tree.

Mountain Alder

Small tree seldom more than 25 feet tall. Small, cone-like fruit persistent until early spring.

Arizona Alder

Larger than Mountain Alder. Leaves more elongated. Fruit similar.

Outdoor Survival

Within recent years, on a Saturday in mid-winter, a retired couple from Iowa drove from their retirement home in Scottsdale, Arizona, to an area about 80 miles northwest of Phoenix on a one-day rock hunting trip.

At this point their pickup truck bogged down in sand on a non-maintained road. The following afternoon the husband (age 74) set out on foot to seek help. Monday morning some hunters discovered the man's body and a subsequent autopsy determined that the cause of death was a heart attack.

An air search located the pickup on Tuesday and the wife (76) was found by sheriff's officers Wednesday about five miles from the vehicle. She was, according to a newspaper article, "conscious but incoherent."

Although this sort of thing happens infrequently, it is a prime example of the trouble that people can encounter almost anywhere, if they are not prepared. This couple made three basic errors:

1. They apparently had not told anyone of their plans and, therefore, they were not considered missing.

2. They had not prepared for a possible extended stay away from civilization, since their food and water consisted of a few sandwiches and apples and one quart of coffee.

3. Obviously they had not educated themselves in the simple fundamentals of survival in, in this case, the Sonoran Desert.

Survival items that EVERY recreational traveler should have in the vehicle:

1. Water. One or more plastic jugs of potable water. These should hold at least one gallon each and can serve for drinking or for vehicle radiator water.

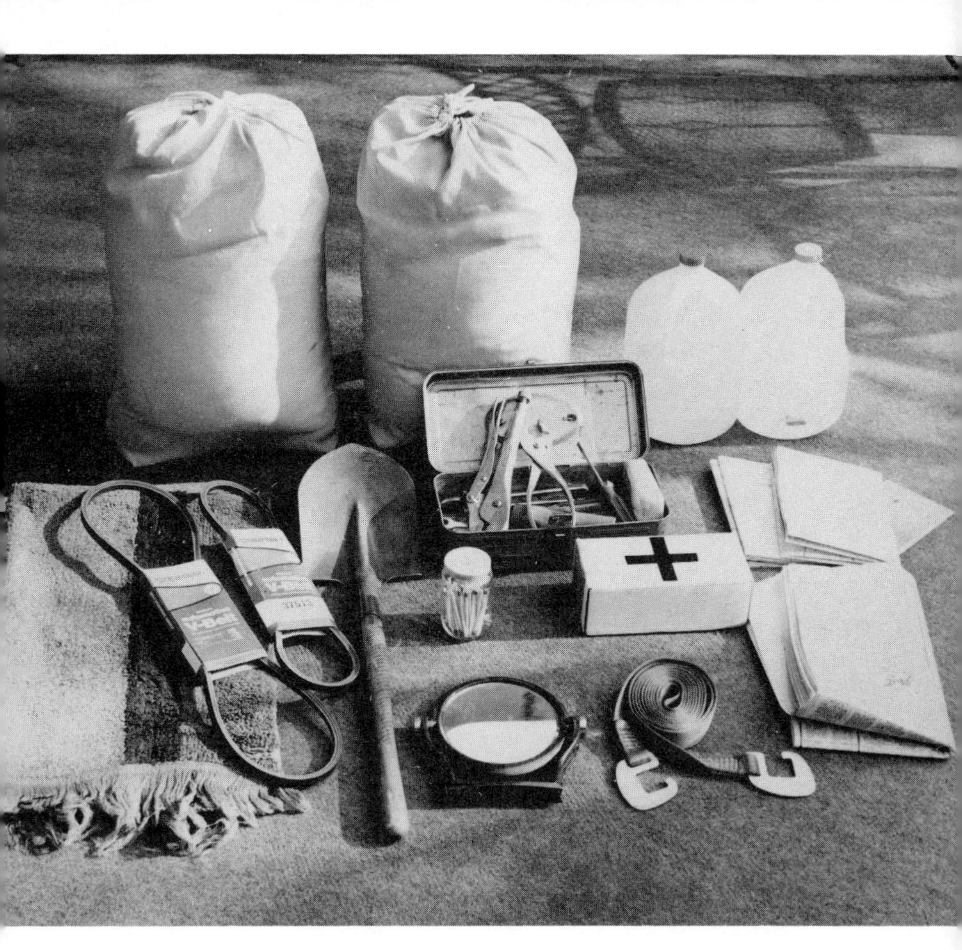

Some of the easily-obtained items that could mean the difference between life and death in a survival situation: old rug, fan belts, shovel, mirror, tow strap, newspaper, maps, first aid kit, matches, tool kit, sleeping bags, water.

2. Tool kit. A small box containing two screwdrivers (Phillips and ordinary), two pairs of pliers (slip joint and vise grip), a set of open-end wrenches, and a roll of electrical tape. The tape is quite handy for, among other things, temporarily stopping a radiator hose leak. Even though you may not have the ability to use the tools to make simple repairs, someone who happens along possibly could.

3. First aid kit. This can be a commercial kit from the drug store or one that you assemble based on the contents of your home medicine chest.

4. Sleeping bags. Ideally, one for each person on the trip. Handy (and could be a lifesaver) if you are stranded overnight almost anywhere. More about this later.

5. Maps. Good maps of the areas you visit are essential. The Iowa man mentioned earlier needed a detail map; he had walked 12 miles but was only five miles from his pickup when found!

ADDITIONAL items for the back roads explorer:

1. More water. At least one gallon per person per day in arid climates. This includes portions of Arizona, California, Colorado, Idaho, Kansas, Montana, North Dakota, Nebraska, New Mexico, Nevada, Oklahoma, Oregon, South Dakota, Texas, Utah, Washington and Wyoming.

2. Snakebite kit. Most of these are of the "cut and suck" kind and, unless they are used quickly and expertly, probably do little good. Very few people in North America ever die from the bite of a poisonous snake. The best treatment is to keep the victim cool, calm and quiet and get him to medical attention as soon as possible. Any exertion on the part of the victim speeds the transport of venom through the body. Cooling the affected part is helpful but care must be taken not to reduce the temperature of the tissue to the point that permanent damage might occur.

3. Newspapers or *white cloth.* To attract the attention of or signal to searching aircraft.

4. Shovel, car jack and an *old rug* or *carpeting.* When your car is stuck in sand, gravel or mud, these are helpful for jacking up the dug-in wheel, excavating an incline or filling a hole, and giving the driving wheel traction to move the vehicle. The small, army type entrenching shovel is ideal.

5. Compass. To help in reading maps and to find directions if you are forced to hike out.

*6. **Boots*** or ***sturdy shoes.*** Be prepared to walk even though your travel plans do not include a hike.

*7. **Matches.*** For starting warming or signal fires. Pile on green brush to make smoke for daytime signaling.

*8. **Mirror.*** A small mirror can be used to signal aircraft or ground vehicles or simply attract the attention of whoever might be out there.

*9. **Tow rope*** or ***chain.***

10. Fan belts. A broken fan belt can be most troublesome. Even though you may not have the tools or ability to replace a belt yourself, someone else may be able to do it for you if you have one of the proper size. Fan belts come in so many different sizes that sometimes it is difficult to find one to fit your car at a remote garage or service station. It is a good policy to have replacement belts in the car at all times. You can drive the car without fan belts but care must be taken to stop and let the engine cool when the temperature gets in the high range or the red light comes on.

11. CB radio. A citizen's band radio is not essential but can be very helpful in emergencies.

Survival often depends upon what people DO or DO NOT DO:

DO let someone know where you are going and when you expect to return. This can be a relative, neighbor, friend or local law enforcement agencies. No one is going to search for you if your absence is not apparent. Lacking all else, leave a written itinerary in a conspicuous place in your home. In public accommodations, leave it with the manager or desk clerk with instructions to notify the authorities if you are several hours overdue.

DO educate yourselves about survival. Many libraries, bookstores and gift shops stock books and pamphlets on the subject that go far beyond the material in this short section. Many of these are produced by local individuals, agencies or organizations familiar with the area.

DO properly equip yourself. Water often is of vital importance in arid regions. A person can get along for several weeks without food, but without water, survival time may be as little as 24 hours under extreme conditions of heat and low humidity and if the individual is forced to walk a long distance. Temperature, wind velocity, humidity, available shade and bodily activity are variables that produce a survival range of from one to nine or 10 days without any water at all.

DO stay with your vehicle whenever possible. This is especially important if someone knows that you may be in trouble. A car or pickup is much easier to find than a human seeking shade under a tree or shrub. If it is necessary to leave your vehicle, try to indicate to searchers when you left and the direction taken. The vehicle offers shade and shelter and, if properly supplied, is your life support system until you are located.

DO try to always know where you are. Watch for landmarks as you drive in and be alert for forks in the road and the general compass direction in which you are traveling. This will make it much easier if you find it necessary to walk out along the same route but in the opposite direction. Try to have adequate maps of the area and use them as you progress.

DO drink enough water to prevent dehydration. Strictly rationing the available water sometimes is not wise if it will lead to heat exhaustion or dehydration. Again, conservation of energy to minimize water loss from the body is more effective than limiting water intake if the supply is not critically low.

DO NOT attempt to drink the vehicle radiator "water." Almost every car and truck now has the radiator filled with a coolant solution of at least 50 percent ethylene glycol. Less than one cup of this liquid causes death in adults.

DO NOT run the car engine and heater if you are trapped in a blizzard. Only when the underneath part of the vehicle is completely clear of snow should the engine and heater be operated for very short periods of time. The danger of possible carbon monoxide build-up inside the car should never be ignored. Here is where the sleeping bags are important. Modern synthetic fiber or down-filled bags are very efficient; they will conserve the body heat of a person and prevent freezing for long periods of time, even at very low temperatures. They are well worth the money and, among other things, make a fine comforter for your bed when unzipped and opened out. Stay inside the sleeping bag inside the car until the storm subsides or help arrives.

DO NOT unnecessarily exert yourself in an arid or high temperature situation. Stay in the shade as much as possible. An opened sleeping bag can be rigged to supply cooler shade than you will find inside the vehicle. Also, a sleeping bag will insulate your body from the hot ground and is a comfortable place to rest. If you must attempt to hike out, do so in late afternoon and early evening and morning. Rest during the hotter portion of the day. Walking at night is not advisable unless you are quite certain of where you are going and can see the terrain.

DO NOT camp, park or picnic in dry washes or other drainages subject to flash flooding. Do not assume that flash floods are confined to the desert southwest; flash floods can occur almost anywhere. Recall the disasters at Rapid City, South Dakota, and the Big Thompson Canyon, Colorado, in recent years. Flash floods can take place when there is not a cloud visible in the sky. Local thunderstorms miles away at the upper reaches of a drainage system are all that is necessary. If you are ever caught in this situation, do not try to drive your car out of the way of an advancing wall of water; run to the nearest high ground.

DO NOT PANIC. Panic has killed more people than sunstroke, freezing and rattlesnakes combined. Try to remain calm and remember what you have learned about survival. Sitting still in the shade or in your blizzard-bound car and thinking about your alternatives uses much less energy than rushing about hysterically.

General view of Sonoran desert vegetation. Notice that the plants are relatively widely spaced due to the very limited amount of water available to individuals.

Appendix A

Suggested Sources of Additional Information

GENERAL

Angier, Bradford and Peter J. Whitney, ***At Home In The Desert,*** Stackpole Books.

Brown, Vinson, ***The Amateur Naturalist's Handbook,*** Little, Brown and Company, Boston.

Collins, Henry Hill, Jr., ***Complete Field Guide to American Wildlife,*** Harper and Row, New York.

Dodge, Natt N. and Herbert S. Zim, ***The Southwest,*** Golden Press, New York.

Heatwole, Thelma, ***Arizona Off The Beaten Path,*** Golden West Publishers, Phoenix.

Jaeger, Edmund C., ***Desert Wildlife,*** Stanford University Press.

Jaques, H. E., ***Living Things and How to Know Them,*** William C. Brown, Dubuque, Iowa.

Laun, H. Charles, ***The Natural History Guide,*** Alsace, Alton, Illinois.

Lowe, Charles H., ***Arizona's Natural Environment,*** University of Arizona Press, Tucson.

McGinnies, William G., ***Discovering the Desert,*** University of Arizona Press.

ANIMALS

Burt, William H., ***Field Guide to the Mammals,*** Houghton Mifflin Co.

Dodge, Natt, ***Poisonous Dwellers of the Desert,*** Southwestern Monuments Association, Globe, Arizona.

Gabrielson, Ira and Herbert S. Zim, ***Birds,*** Golden Press, New York.

Morgan, Ann, ***Field Book of Ponds and Streams,*** G. P. Putnam's Sons, New York.

Murie, Olas, ***A Field Guide to Animal Tracks,*** Houghton Mifflin, Boston.

Olin, George, ***Animals of the Southwest Deserts,*** Southwestern Monuments Association, Globe, Arizona.

Olin, George, ***Mammals of the Southwest Mountains and Mesas,*** Southwestern Monuments Association, Globe, Arizona.

Peterson, Roger, ***A Field Guide to the Birds*** and ***A Field Guide to the Western Birds,*** Houghton Mifflin Co., Boston.

Zim, Herbert S. and Clarence Cottam, ***Insects,*** Golden Press, NY

Zim, Herbert S. and D. F. Hoffmeister, ***Mammals,*** Golden Press, NY

Zim, Herbert S. and H. M. Smith, ***Reptiles and Amphibians,*** Golden Press, NY.

PLANTS

Armstrong, Margaret, ***Field Book of Western Flowers,*** G. P. Putnam's Sons, New York.

Arnberger, Leslie P., ***Flowers of the Southwest Mountains,*** Southwestern Monuments Association, Globe, Arizona.

Baerg, Harry, ***How to Know the Western Trees,*** William C. Brown Co., Dubuque, Iowa.

Benson, Lyman, ***The Cacti of Arizona,*** University of Arizona Press.

Crittenden, Mabel, ***Trees of the West,*** Celestial Arts, Millbrae, California.

Dodge, Natt N., ***Flowers of the Southwest Deserts,*** Southwestern Monuments Association, Globe, Arizona.

Foxx, Teralenes and Dorothy Hoard, ***Flowers of the Southwestern Forests and Woodlands,*** Los Alamos Historical Society.

Little, Elbert, ***Southwestern Trees,*** U.S. Department of Agriculture, Washington, DC.

Patraw, Pauline M., ***Flowers of the Southwest Mesas,*** Southwestern Monuments Association, Globe, Arizona.

Petrides, George A., ***A Field Guide to Trees and Shrubs,*** Houghton Mifflin, Boston.

Pohl, R. W., ***How to Know the Grasses,*** William C. Brown Company, Dubuque, Iowa.

GEOLOGY

Anthony, John W., et al, ***Mineralogy of Arizona,*** University of Arizona Press, Tucson.

Arizona Bureau of Mines, ***Mineral and Water Resources of Arizona,*** University of Arizona, Tucson.

Chronic, Halka, ***Roadside Geology of Arizona,*** Mountain Press Publishing Company.

Loomis, Frederic, ***Field Book of Common Rocks and Minerals,*** G. P. Putnam's Sons, New York.

Mardirosian, Charles A., ***Mining Districts and Mineral Deposits of Arizona (map and data sheet),*** Mineral Research Company, P.O. Box 11427, Albuquerque, NM.

Rhodes, Frank H. T., et al, ***Fossils,*** Golden Press, New York.

Wilson, Eldred, ***A Resume of the Geology of Arizona,*** University of Arizona Press, Tucson.

Zim, Herbert S. and Paul R. Shaffer, ***Rocks and Minerals,*** Golden Press, New York.

Appendix B

Common Rocks and Minerals of Arizona

MINERALS

Calcite ($CaCO_3$). Occurs mostly as cave formations. Crystalline, soft—can be scratched with fingernail. Effervesces strongly with hydrochloric acid (HCl), weakly with vinegar.

Caliche ($CaCO_3$). Commonly formed as a secondary deposit of calcium carbonate. Whitish, soft. Effervesces with acid. Found extensively on rocks and in soils of Basin and Range province.

Chalcedony (SiO_2). Translucent, waxy form of quartz. White to red. Forms desert "buttons" or "roses" and fire agate. Usually found in association with volcanic rock in many localities.

Cinnebar (HgS). Principal ore of mercury. Pink to deep red. Occurs prominently in quartz and schistose rocks of Mazatzal Mountains.

Feldspar (Potassium, sodium or calcium aluminum silicates). Ordinarily found as a component of granite. Color varies from almost colorless to white, pink and buff. Weathers from granite as squarish crystals with flat surfaces. Source of most of the clay in soils.

Gypsum ($CaSO_4$ or $CaSO_4 \cdot 2H_2O$). White to pearly colorless. Fibrous or crystalline. Very soft, easily scratched with fingernail.

Hematite (Fe_2O_3). Dark brown or black compact, heavy mineral. Occurs as small, irregular masses in Mountain and Transition provinces.

Hornblende (Hydrous silicates of calcium, iron and magnesium). Dark crystals occur in many kinds of igneous rocks.

Jasper (SiO_2). Bright red to reddish brown. Opaque. Often with milky quartz veins. Found widely in gravelly areas in Mountain and Colorado Plateau provinces.

Magnetite (Fe_3O_4). Magnetic iron oxide. Occurs as black sand in desert washes. Can be picked up with a magnet.

Mica (Aluminum silicate with other metallic elements). Thin sheets that are colorless to black. Found in granites, schists, pegmatites and gneisses.

Quartz (SiO_2). Occurs in many forms and colors due principally to mode of origin and included impurities. Pure quartz is colorless and crystalline as the clear crystals ("diamonds") found in parts of the Transition province.

Tourmaline (Aluminum silicate with boron, iron and sodium). Commonly black but may be other dark colors. Long triangular crystals often found in Basin and Range pegmatites.

Travertine ($CaCO_3$). The form that calcium carbonate takes when precipitated on the surface from the waters of springs and geysers. (See Tonto Natural Bridge)

•

SEDIMENTARY ROCKS

Breccia. A conglomerate consisting of angular fragments cemented together.

Chert (SiO_2 with $CaCO_3$). Found in association with limestones. Frequently banded. Color varies from white to black plus yellow and buff. Common in limestones of Transition and Colorado Plateau provinces. Prehistoric Indians used this material, among others, in manufacturing weapons and implements.

Conglomerate. A conglomeration of rounded stones that may range from sand grains to boulders, cemented together with any one of several possible substances.

Desert patina. Dark deposit on most desert country rocks not situated in the lower parts of washes, streams or rivers. Dew and rain bring iron and other dark minerals to the surface of the rock where they are left when the water evaporates. There is not enough rainfall in arid regions to remove these accumulations.

Limestone. Principally calcium carbonate but with a variety of possible impurities leading to a wide range of colors and textures. Frequently fossiliferous. Effervesces with acids. Occur extensively in the Transition and Colorado Plateau provinces.

Sandstone. Consists of sand grains cemented together. Feels sandy to the touch. Extensive formations in Transition and Colorado Plateau provinces.

Shale. Compacted and/or cemented particles of clay (see Feldspar). Occurs frequently in association with limestone and sandstone formations. Dendrites often are found on the flat surfaces of shale. These are pseudofossils formed by manganese compounds left behind when water containing them in solution left or was absorbed by the shale. Dendrites resemble plant fossils and are seen in other rocks than shale.

●

IGNEOUS ROCKS

Andesite. Volcanic rock intermediate in composition between rhyolite and basalt.

Basalt. Rich in metallic oxides. Occurs in a variety of colors whose shades can range from very light to very dark. Forms massive intrusions and lava flows. Very common in Arizona. Crystalls usually too small to be detected with the unaided eye.

Dacite. Compacted, welded volcanic fragments ordinarily of small size (ashes and cinders). Forms layers or masses of varying color and shade. The main Superstition Mountain range is largely dacite.

Granite. Rich in siliceous minerals (quartz, feldspars). Generally consists of mixtures of several kinds of relatively large crystals. Usually light in color and of lower density than basaltic rocks. Widely distributed in Basin and Range and Mountain provinces.

Pegmatite. Granitic rock in which the crystals are much larger than in ordinary granite. Often found in mountainous areas as vertical intrusions (dikes).

Rhyolite. Chemically similar to granite but crystals are very small. Often occurs as lava flows and sometimes as small intrusions. Seen in scattered localities in the Transition province, among others.

●

METAMORPHIC ROCKS

Chlorite schist. Iron-aluminum and magnesium silicates. Greenish in color. Schists consist of fine, flaky particles and are named for the principal mineral.

Gneiss. Different minerals are in layers or roughly parallel bands rather than being intermixed as in the original rock (such as granite). Resembles some schists but texture is crystalline rather than flaky.

Quartzite. Metamorphosed sandstone. Sand grains no longer apparent. Rock now has crystalline structure or is much harder than the original sandstone and breaks through the particles rather than around them. Some quartzite is easily mistaken for granite.

Slate. Altered shale. Blue or purplish to black, sometimes green or red. Much harder than most shale; difficult or impossible to break with hands.

Talc schist. Talc is magnesium silicate. The schist is white or yellowish or, if it contains cinnabar, it may be pink or red. If there is enough talc present, the rock surface feels smooth or oily to the touch.

Appendix C

The Pyramid of Life

Without exception, every plant and every animal in the world is dependent to some degree upon other living organisms and, of course, upon the physical environment in which each exists. This is illustrated in the Pyramid of Life diagram. Note that the pyramid's foundation consists of a complex of solar energy, soil, air and water; all of which are required by green plants, the basic producers in any ecosystem. Without green plants, almost none of the other forms of life could exist. Even in a small area (a microhabitat) of any of the communities, one will find examples of these principles.

The delicate balances involving interdependences and interactions of producers, herbivores, carnivores and decomposers and their habitats are seldom suspected by the casual human invader. It behooves us, then, to tread with caution lest we radically disturb this balance of nature. The displacement or removal of any part of a habitat (a stick or stone, leaf, twig or animal) could cause serious consequences to the denizens of the microhabitat concerned.

Even more serious consequences are effected by larger scale disruptions resulting from the works of man: roads, power lines, pipe lines, dams, buildings, logging, overkilling and people driving off-road vehicles. Our mere presence often is enough to create problems. We are told that the stately saguaro cactus soon will be gone from the vicinity of Phoenix and Tucson simply because great numbers of people live and carry on their ordinary activities in these cities. How can the simple existence of a million humans cause the local eradication of a million cacti? How this happens is a significant lesson in ecology.

When people move into an area, some animals move out—especially the predators such as coyotes, foxes, bobcats, hawks, owls and eagles. When this happens, the rodent population explodes to the point that competition for food becomes extreme. The rodents are thus forced to eat things not usually on their menus—things such as young saguaro cacti. When old cacti die off (as all elderly forms of life do) there are few or no young ones to replace them. Other factors accelerate the process: overgrazing by man's domestic animals, hunting and trapping of predators almost completely unprotected by game laws, and crushing of young cacti under the relentless wheels of off-road vehicles.

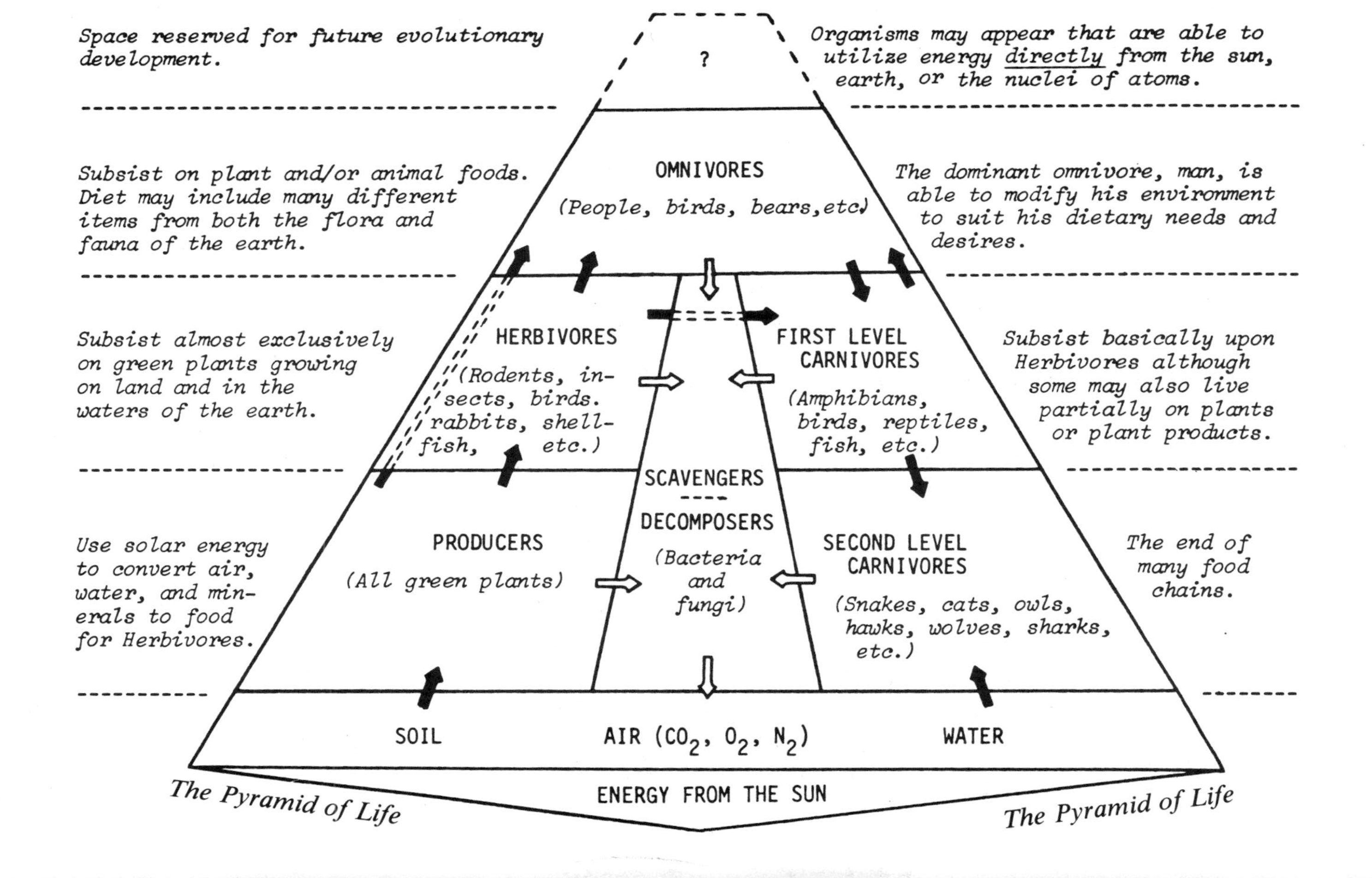

The Pyramid of Life

Index

D

E

F

G

H

O

P

Q

R

S

T

U

V

W

Y

Z

Order from your book dealer or direct from publisher.

ORDER BLANK

Golden West Publishers

4113 N. Longview Ave.
Phoenix, AZ 85014

Please ship the following books:

_______ Arizona Outdoor Guide ($5.00)

_______ Arizona Museums ($5.00)

_______ Arizona Adventure ($5.00)

_______ Arizona—off the Beaten Path ($4.50)

_______ Arizona Cook Book ($3.50)

_______ California Favorites ($3.50)

_______ Chili-Lovers' Cook Book ($3.50)

_______ Citrus Recipes ($3.50)

_______ Fools' Gold (Lost Dutchman Mine) ($5.00)

_______ Ghost Towns in Arizona ($4.50)

_______ Greater Phoenix Street Maps Book ($4.00)

_______ How to Succeed in Selling Real Estate ($3.50)

_______ London Theatre Today ($4.50)

_______ Mexican Cook Book ($5.00)

I enclose $ __________ (including $1 per order postage, handling).

Name ____

Address ____

City ______________________ State ______ Zip________

This order blank may be photo copied

Books from Golden West Publishers

Read of the daring deeds and exploits of Wyatt Earp, Buckey O'Neill, the Rough Riders, Arizona Rangers, cowboys, Power brothers shootout, notorious Tom Horn, Pleasant Valley wars, "first" American revolution—action-packed true tales of early Arizona! ***Arizona Adventure (by Marshall Trimble), 160 pages . . . $5.00.***

The lost hopes, the lost lives—the lost gold! Facts, myths and legends of the Lost Dutchman Gold Mine and the Superstition Mountains. Told by a geologist who was there! ***Fools' Gold (by Robert Sikorsky), 144 pages . . . $5.00.***

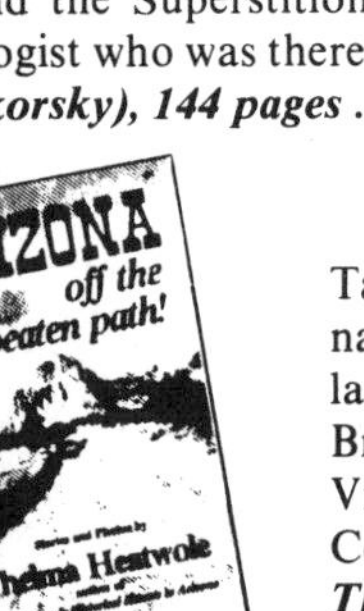

Take the back roads to and thru Arizona's natural wonders—Canyon de Chelly, Wonderland of Rocks, Monument Valley, Rainbow Bridge, Four Peaks, Swift Trail, Alamo Lake, Virgin River Gorge, Palm Canyon, Red Rock Country! ***Arizona—off the beaten path! (by Thelma Heatwole), 144 pages . . . $4.50.***

A taste of the Old Southwest, from sizzling Indian fry bread to prickly pear marmalade, from spicy pinto beans to outdoor barbecuing. ***Arizona Cook Book (by Al and Mildred Fischer), 144 pages . . . $3.50.***

Visit the silver cities of Arizona's golden past with this prize-winning reporter-photographer. Come along to the towns whose heydays were once wild and wicked! See crumbling adobe walls, old mines, cemeteries, cabins and castles. ***Ghost Towns and Historical Haunts in Arizona (by Thelma Heatwole), 144 pages . . . $4.50.***

Arizona Museums—See them all! More than 175 fascinating museums, zoos, botanical gardens and art centers are described and photographed in this up-do-date volume, complete with maps. ***Arizona Museums (by Al and Mildred Fischer), 88 large pages . . . $5.00.***